HOW TO
AWAKEN THE POWER
WITHIN YOU

HABITS TO A HEALTHIER, HAPPIER, MORE PROSPEROUS YOU

DIANA DOLCE
AWARD WINNING AUTHOR

HOW TO AWAKEN THE POWER WITHIN YOU

Publisher
10-10-10 Publishing
Markham, ON
Canada

Printed in the United States of America

DEDICATION

I dedicate this book to my Grandpa Biagio. I am sorry I never had the honor to meet you. You have always been in my thoughts. Those thoughts put me on this journey, to try to seek the answers of *why?* and *how?*

In 1938, there was a bad train accident, my grandpa got hit by a train and never made it home to his wife and 2 sons. My dad at the time was 4 years old; his brother was less than a year old. My dad would always go with his father to pick up the newspaper and have ice cream after dinner. The story was told, one night, my dad didn't go with my grandpa because of bad weather. I am grateful my dad wasn't with him. I don't truly know whether it was an accident or intentional; it was said, to be an accident. What I do know today is that your thoughts, your words, and your actions, create your outcomes.

I also dedicate this book to all of you who believe your current circumstances dictate the program of the rest of your life; you may feel helpless and hopeless; you could never get ahead; you suffer from a "dis/ease" within your body; you feel alone; you feel like an addiction has taken over you; you feel you need to accept life as it is. Refute all those thoughts! They are only true if you allow them to be true. You may be going through a bad chapter; it's not your whole book. You are a spiritual being having a human experience.

I was destined to write this book to give you the answer of "why and how" you attract the life you have.

I have a message for you:

"The Power Within You . . . is Greater than any Circumstance Around You!"

Don't accept your current circumstances; don't put energy on anything you don't want. If you don't want to own them . . . Refute them! There is a trained way of thinking and speaking to create the outcomes you want, you will learn the "how to" from this book. You will start planting the right seeds to create and manifest the life you want.

Today is a new page to the rest of your book.

THE CONTENTS OF POWER

ACKNOWLEDGEMENTS

I want to Thank you, God, and all the angels above, for the continuous guidance and direction you have brought through my life. I always feel your presence and I always walk in faith, knowing you're right with me to fulfill all my life purposes. This book is an acknowledgement of the faith I had to go forth to write this book to get this powerful message out. Writing a book was not in my physical thoughts at all. I wanted to reach the many, with all the knowledge I have accumulated, through the decades of my life. Spirit told me, "to reach the many, you need to write your own book." My message was louder than my fear. I put total faith in you. You made it fun, easy, and effortless, that is what I claimed before I wrote the book. This book confirmed my spirit is awake. I am ready to awaken others! I am equipped and I am ready for more! "Thy will be Done."

I want to Thank you, Mom and Dad (Maria and Ben), for giving me 3 wonderful brothers, Bobby, Michael, and Eddie, and for teaching us all the values of family. For your selfless acts of love and being the glue to always keep us together. For always being there for all your children, grandchildren, and great grandchildren. For teaching me your work ethics, and saving up enough money to purchase a summer home on the lake, a happy, peaceful place that will continue for generations to bring everyone joy. So many happy memories were made with family and friends at the lake. I am grateful for all the years of reading my wellness books on the paddle boat, which brought me the knowledge to bring forth and continue my work in the world.

I want to Thank you, Den, my dearest, loving husband, for being my love and my support. You are my Ace that I need every day. You help manifest my visions into reality. You have helped me bring the love of our three children, Anthony, Angelo, and Angelica, with an addition of our son-in-law Jonathan, our grandson Paul, and another baby boy on the way, into our lives. You all are the treasures of my life and keep me striving every day for answers to help keep us happier, healthier, and more prosperous for the rest of our lives together as our family grows.

I want to Thank you, all my family and my friends that are like my family, for all the love and support you bring me, the fun times, the challenging times, the memories we have shared and will continue to share, that makes life even more meaningful.

I want to Thank you, Lightwing Center of LifeSpirit Congregational Church for ordaining me as a Minister Practitioner of Inspirational Healing Center to help inspire and awaken others to the LifeSpirit within; for teaching me the knowledge of the biblical healing oils.

I want to Thank you, Rick Ercolano, for introducing me to Kangen water, "God's living water." This is how I feel about it and I hear so many people say that to me. For all the support you give me and my team of over 120 distributors. You are so full of knowledge and you take so much pride in sharing it. I do hope Kangen is the next major appliance in everyone's home.

I want to Thank you, Dr. Billy Geris, for all your knowledge as a doctor, to help me see fully the two sides of the coin—the sickness industry that you have studied and the wellness industry that I have studied. We have really been able to compliment each other. I hope one day to see the sickness industry utilizing the wellness industry much more than it is.

I want to Thank you, Mary Morrissey, my mentor, my coach, my inspiration to believe in my own beliefs. You helped me turn up the volume to my inner self, to really listen for what I needed to pay attention to, and you helped me turn off the voices that say, "You can't." I am so grateful for becoming a Dream Builder coach, so I may help others manifest their dreams. The Brave Thinking Mastery Class really put me over the edge in utilizing my own thinking, and I highly recommend it for everyone. To me, it is the utmost importance to master your own thinking. When you master your thinking, you master your life.

I want to Thank you, Dr. Corinne Allen, for all the knowledge you have brought me about the Kangen Ionized Alkaline Water and the Young Living Essential oils, as well as for all the studies that you have performed and brought to me through cds, dvds, and books that you have recommended. I hope one of these days I can intern with you at your Brain Advance Center in Idaho. You are packed with so much knowledge, and I am so grateful for you sharing it. God bless you with all your work and your continued studies for Brain Advancement.

I want to Thank you, the deceased, Dr. Batmanghelidj; although you are no longer here, your knowledge and work lives on. I have received so much knowledge from your books and cds that I have shared about the vital importance of water; you have confirmed my beliefs and I hope to continue to bring this message out. Water is essential for all of life.

I want to Thank you, Raymond Aaron, your "Get Your Book Done" 10-10-10 Program, and your staff, for making this book a reality. It was never in my thoughts to write a book until

I met you. You truly inspired me and sparked something inside. You made it fun, easy, and effortless for me to bring out the message that was inside me. The boot camp in Florida was a great help and I was ready to get my book into editing in 6 weeks. I highly recommend this program for anyone, if you're serious about getting your book done. I want to thank my book architect, Rosa Greco and Liz Ventrella, for all their guidance and encouragement, and for keeping me on track for my deadline.

I want to Thank you, everyone that I know that that has touched my life in some way, there are too many of you to mention, I love you all.   xoxo

FOREWORD

I am delighted to present to you, *How to Awaken The Power Within You*. This book is jam packed with an abundance of wisdom, knowledge and inspiration that will leave you feeling powerful! Diana Dolce has put together this guide to help awaken you to a new habitual way of thinking, speaking, acting, loving, breathing, drinking, eating, exercising and attracting money, all while you are walking in faith.

What separates this book from any other motivational book out on the market is that Diana demonstrates to you exactly how you can achieve your goals to live a healthier, happier and more prosperous life. Diana has over 45 years of life experience mastering her own power within herself, and she uses her knowledge to show you how you can do the same. Diana has postulated love, good health, good friends, happiness and prosperity into her life, and she is unleashing her secrets within these very pages so that you, too, can attain all of your life desires.

Diana truly paves the path for you to see the light in your life and I know that she will inspire and motivate you to start your incredible life changing journey of awakening the power within you today.

—Raymond Aaron
New York Times Best Selling Author

TESTIMONIALS

Diana . . . is a Light and spreads her Light to Enlighten.

—Lori Giraldo, Staten Island, NY

Diana is more than just an ordinary friend. She reaches the spirituality in your soul. She lights a fire in you so you know that there is nothing in your life that thru the power of God within you, you cannot overcome. Her amazing selflessness, strength, and spiritual energy is truly admiring. She is like the energizer battery carried with angel wings. I cannot say enough about how much I admire this remarkable woman for all she does. God bless you, Diana, keep Hope alive!

—Rita, Staten Island, NY

I have known Diana over 30 years and found her to be a very inspirational, caring, outgoing, considerate, generous, and loving person. She always tries to find the good in everything and sends positive energy into the world. I am blessed that she is a part of my life and love her dearly.

—Evelyn Arrigo, Staten Island, NY

Diana has always been there for me, lifting my spirits with her kind caring words, inspirational talks and, most of all, her genuine friendship.

—Eileen C., Island Park, NY

A must read! I have known Diana Dolce for many years . . . Her knowledge and her philosophies are to be paid attention to!

—Ilene Reichman, Esq., Queens, New York

Diana Dolce is a "Triple Treat!" for powering up your MIND, BODY and SOUL. Her positive reinforcement, caring and keen insight helped me awaken all three and get back on my feet. Her book will do the same for you.

—Robert Steele, Staten Island, NY

"Listen to my Wife". . . she knows what she is talking about . . . it took me years to understand this . . . I don't think I would be here if it wasn't for her . . . I am so grateful for her . . . "I Love You, Diana."

—Dennis Dolce, Husband, Staten Island, NY

Inspirational, positive and confident is how you will feel after reading this book. Diana Dolce doesn't only teach how to change your thoughts but she lives it. She teaches us about how good things can and will happen by willing it to yourself and being thankful for it when it happens. You will learn and become aware of what is toxic in your life, and you will switch your channel to a higher and more positive one. Thank you, Diana for spreading the positivity!

—Lisa DiGennaro, Realtor, Staten Island, New York

Diana's advice with health, mindset, and the benefits of water intake (Kangen) are 110%. I have known Diana for 30+ years, and she has always been an energetic and loving, caring person; she is the sister I never had. She believes in moving and never staying idle; she cares so much about health, fitness, and how the body takes care of itself. Her advice changed my life. I suffer from reflux and took over-the-counter antacids practically on a daily basis, but since Diana has always taken a huge interest in helping people like myself by bringing them water and teaching the benefit of essential oils versus medication, she has changed my life for the better. My reflux has diminished and my energy levels have increased. I'm not getting sick as often with her advice on supplements, such as Juice Plus. I'm a true fan and believer in what she is going to achieve; her kind heart and determination will help many. God Bless you, Diana Dolce. Love you as my best friend/sister always.

—Marie Agosta, Staten Island, New York

The day I met Diana Dolce, an angel walked into my life. She was cheerful, kind, and understanding. In a dark chapter in my life, she introduced Kangen water. I was suffering from psoriasis and IBS as my boyfriend was lying in bed suffering from kidney failure. Diana was supportive and sincerely concerned about my health and my boyfriend's. As I started drinking the water, my psoriasis vanished and has never returned, in addition, the IBS that was taunting me for years went away! I now live a healthier, happier life thanks to Diana taking an interest in my wellness. Thank you!

—Alyson Cinquemani, Fitness Professional, Manahawkin, NJ

Diana, you have been a Huge Positive Inspiration to me, you walk the walk, Upbeat, Healthy, and a Beautiful Soul. So, glad I met you.

—Linda Poplardo, Houston TX

Diana is a most inspiring soul. She gives straight from her heart; she loves dearly and deeply . . . God bless her.

—Susan G Chamberlain, PhD, Intuitive Healer, New York

Diana . . . thank you for being the positive role model in my life. You never judge or say anything negative. The world needs more people like you in it. God bless you!

—Valerie Casertano, Staten Island, NY

Diana . . . thank you for inspiring us with your words and recommendations and for always giving us positive energy.

—Loretta, Tommy & Lisa, Staten Island, NY

All I can say is Kangen Water is God's water . . . it makes you feel good, healthy, and energetic. It helps the body heal itself! It is God's gift to the world. I thank you, Diana, for introducing the water to me, and for all you do for everyone.

—Carmine Amarando, Staten Island, NY

Having Diana as a friend is an excellent example of friendship in itself. Open-minded, genuine, compassionate, and level-headed, she can always be counted on to listen and provide support when needed. Her wonderful sense of humor, adventure, and life experiences have given her the ability to see any situation in a positive sense. Personally, believing that "people come into our lives for a reason, a season, or a lifetime," I've known for a long time that Diana is a lifetime friend.

—Gene Phillips, Manahawkin, NJ

One thing I can say about Diana is that she always has a smile on her face. She has a positive outlook that could encourage anyone!! She is a trooper . . . a strong woman . . . a wonderful friend . . . I love taking her X-Halates class, and I love her, even more. She is a friend, forever.

—Jean Zagame, Group Fitness Coordinator, SI, NY

I have known Diana Dolce for more than 12 years, and there is one word that comes to my mind when I think about her . . . Positivity. Diana embraces the whole meaning of this word and puts it into her reality by living by it. I think those who read her book will gain insight and feel inspired to look for a direction which will bring the same positivity and focus that you all desire.

—Valerie Murphy, Staten Island, NY

Ms. Dolce has a lovely personality . . . she conducts an outstanding and inspirational class every time!

—Pat Q, JCC, SI,NY

Diana encourages me and makes me feel healthy and happy . . . she inspires me to do better . . . she is my favorite instructor.

—Patsey Caso, JCC, SI,NY

Diana helped me get better with chair yoga . . . I can move a lot easier now.

—Mary Rubino, JCC, SI, NY

Diana is gracious, generous and loving . . . a blessing in my life . . . love her, sister in Christ.

—Liz, Staten Island, NY

I am so grateful Diana is as persistent as she is. I was diagnosed with Lyme Disease in July 2014. Dating back to 2003-2004 (when my symptoms began) I was seen by several different doctors. My body began to slow down. I complained of chronic joint pain, numbing in my arms and hands and as time went on I began to develop large "nodules" on my fingers. I eventually lost strength in both hands. Simple everyday tasks became difficult. I could no longer button, zipper, or hold anything in either hand (gallon of milk etc.) without supporting it with my other hand. My legs were weak, I suffered with severe migraines and at times just couldn't get out of bed. Doctor after doctor, they all said the same thing . . . "no nerve damage, no carpal tunnel, no rheumatoid arthritis." I eventually found my way to an Infectious Disease Specialist in New Jersey. Blood was drawn and two weeks later, I was told that I tested positive for Lyme Disease. I began taking Biaxin (500MG 2x's a day), Monodox (100MG 2x's a day) and Diflucan(100MG 1x a day) for several months. My symptoms began to worsen. I was told it was the "toxins" in my body fighting the medications. I was switched to Alinia (500MG 3x's a day). Once again, the pain was unbearable. Diana, being my neighbor kept saying try the Kangen water, she would constantly bring me over gallons to drink up.

After reading about the "benefits" of the water, the testimonials, and going to a demonstration I decided to invest in a machine. I purchased the SD501 Platinum series. I stopped all meds (against doctor's wishes) and began drinking the water. On average, I drink 72 to 96 ounces a day. I also eliminated "junk food" and began eating a healthier diet. Today, March 2017, I can honestly say I feel great! I noticed a dramatic difference in my skin, nails, and hair. I went back to exercising (4-5x's a week) and must say, I have more strength and stamina now than I've had in years! I love my water and I am grateful for this amazing technology. I just want you to know that for me, the water has made a world of difference for me and my family, Thank you a bunch Diana!

—Kathleen S, Staten Island, NY

AUTHOR'S NOTE...

I am grateful and happy you have a copy of my book in your hands. It shows me that you have a longing for a healthier, happier, more prosperous life. You are forever evolving into existence, more and more revolutionized ways; it starts and ends with you. You have the power and the choice to make the rest of your life be the best of your life. I am here to shed light upon all your power, to help you awaken your gifts, so you may utilize them to bring joy to your life. You have everything you need to manifest everything you want.

"The doctor of the future will give no medicine but instead will interest his patients in the care of the human frame, in diet, and in the cause and prevention of disease."

—Thomas Edison.

The information and recommendations I make in this book is from years of training as a Holistic Health Practitioner, a Fitness Instructor, Personal Trainer, a Dream Builder Coach, a Wellness Coach, a Molecular Hydration Specialist, a Cosmetologist, a Realtor, very extensive research, publications and from personal experiences. I am not a doctor; I am a Holistic Minister Practitioner. My teachings under God are to Awaken your Life Spirit, the Power Within You, to bring yourself to a state of wholeness, ease, and balance. I do not dispense medical advice or prescribe the use or the discontinuance of any medication. Always speak to your own doctor with any medical concerns.

My soul purpose is to bring you an understanding that you have one Creator, and He created you in his like image;

the power that is within Him is within you. You live in an abundant Universe and there is no lack except in your thinking. You have royal blood running through your veins. You need the "Royal Flush" to maintain your royal kingdom. The "*how* to" will be discussed in the book. You are a master creator, and I will help you awaken your own power that you were gifted with. Don't depend on anyone else for your happiness and for your healing. You have the power within you. Refute what you don't want, and create what you do want through vision, thoughts, words, and actions. Habits can't be changed; they can be replaced. I am going to give you the power tools to replace old useless habits for new life giving habits. You "O.W.E." it to yourself. Oxygen, Water, and Enzymes are key essentials for keeping your power alive and kicking! You could be old at 30 or young at 90. It's all in your perception. The words "can't" don't exist. Baby steps could take you all the way up the highest peak. Start taking action now! You could do this! I have faith in you! I believe in you! Believe and love yourself! Take the first step, read this book, chapter by chapter. At the end of each chapter, write power notes to yourself. Read the book a few times, each time you will see it in a different light.

With Love and Light!

Diana

CHAPTER 1

IS YOUR POWER
AWAKE OR ASLEEP?

Are you awake to what life has to offer you? Or, are you sleeping your life away? Are you, taking full advantage of living and designing the life you want to live? The key is: *Want* to live. You have choices. You have unlimited choices and resources. You are a child of the infinite. The Infinite wants to give you the magic lamp to fulfill all your desires and all your needs. Your life, right now, is the result of your thinking, speaking, and actions. The infinite is always at your command. You are an Infinite Spiritual being having a human experience.

I want you to ask yourself, "Do I love my life? Do I like my life? Do I hate my life? What life?" . . . Now, I want you to answer out loud, to yourself, either: "I love my life!; I like my life; I hate my life; or What life?" Depending on how you answered determines if the power within you is awake or if you really need to wake it up. If you answered, "I love my life," then you are living a well-connected life to your source of power. If you answered, "I like my life," then you know there is a source of power, but you are not utilizing it to its fullest potential. If you answered either, "I hate my life" or "What life?," then you are totally asleep to your source of power, you think life happens to you. Life happens through you! There is a reason why you have a copy of my book in your hand. You are destined for more! I am going to give you all the tools that I was guided to share with you to awaken the power that is within you to more and more greatness. "The power within you is greater than any circumstance around you." In life, never stay stagnant, always seek for more, and be grateful every step of the way.

Do you feel like you are traveling life alone? You may feel God is somewhere up there, but, he is too busy taking care of other things. You may feel that you don't want to bother God with your trivial things. The truth is: God is within you and you are of his utmost importance; there is nothing too trivial about any of your needs and wants. You might have been brought up, either by religion or your parents, to not ask for things and to be happy and grateful for what you have. That is partly true. I grew up the same way. I was happy and grateful for what I had, but I kept visioning more of what I would like and my life kept spiraling upward. I will show you how to do the same.

There is something inside you pushing you for more and more. You may have the volume down, or there is too much noise around you to pay attention. God has been there for you and won't leave your side. When things aren't going right, people tend to blame others for their results. Each of us has dominion over our own thoughts, words, and actions, and we are the only ones to blame when things are not going right. You are your own best friend and cheerleader, or you could be your own worst enemy. Are your own thoughts, words, and actions cheering you on to better things or knocking you down with the negative pity parties going on within you? Let's take a dive into your soul. Did you even know you had a soul? You do! We all do—no exceptions! When you connect, and awaken the power within you, there are less, or no more pity parties. Try to inspire pessimists around you and never let them bring you down and never let their words get inside you. Try to inspire them or let them go, don't let them drag you down. Save your good energy. You will build a confidence—a knowing—when you become one with the power within you, your Life Spirit. You will become more and more resilient to the negatives around you. Surround yourself with a positive sphere of influence, master minds of knowing.

Just like in an old time movie favorite, "The Wizard of Oz," when Glenda the good witch says to Dorothy, "You had the power all along my dear . . . You just needed to learn how to use it." Many of you could relate to that statement, and many of you don't know what it means by "your power is asleep." When you are thrown challenges, many times it is a stepping stone to better things. Don't become defeated, what may hurt you, makes you stronger. It is when you weather the storm and come out on the other side not completely defeated that you learn the biggest lessons. You are still here, living and breathing—learn from it. I find there is always a big message inside every storm. Only you know that message. Learn to quiet yourself down and listen to the whisper. Prayer is you talking to God, meditation is God talking to you. Your higher self will always guide you to good. Learn to trust in yourself. Learn to walk in faith. Your self knows best.

If you're not already acquainted with your soul, it's time for me to introduce you to your higher intelligence, which is connected to the infinite. Close your eyes. Notice the tip of your nose, notice your right foot, notice your left pinky, and notice the seat you're sitting in. Now, notice what is noticing that. That is your Life Spirit—your soul that is one with God, Universal Intelligence, and the Infinite. You could call your power anything that you feel comfortable with— God, Jesus, Father, Holy Spirit, Universe, Infinite Intelligence, Messiah, etc.—the important thing is, call upon it. I personally feel connected with my life spirit, and I feel I have lots of angels working in my best interest all the time. It's important that you have faith in your power; that you call upon your power daily, like a best friend or a parent. God wants to know all your longings and your discontents, daily. You really need to say what you want and really want what you say, when you are speaking to your higher self.

Unlike what some religions say, "the Messiah will be coming soon," the Messiah is here! The Messiah is within You! You don't have to wait, you don't need to look any further. God is not something or someone outside you, God, the infinite intelligence is inside you. He created you in his likeness. The love and the peace of God is within you. You have full dominion over your thoughts, your thoughts become things. Awaken!

It is said that the quality of your life depends on the quality of the questions you ask God. Ask lots of good questions. Concentrate on one, especially right before dozing off to sleep. How could I . . . ? Like the saying goes, "Let me sleep on it," has truth behind it. Your higher power will guide you on the right answer when you are truly connected to your source. Learn to in source not out source, the best answer always comes from within.

Are you awake or asleep to the energy in money? Are you blocking the flow? You will learn how to magnetize money, in a future chapter. If there is a certain job you want, ask, "How could I get this job at . . . ?" The more specific you are, the better it is. Ask, "How could I earn an extra $$$$ each week?" I asked, "How could I generate enough money to keep my Inspirational Healing Center flowing and make a difference in the world?" It led me to creating this book that you are reading now. I have to honestly say there was nowhere in my thoughts in the physical realm about writing a book. I personally didn't have the knowing or the confidence in doing it on my own; I didn't even like writing a book report. Something inside me was guiding me for more. Through becoming a Dream Builder coach, I really learned how to listen to my own longings and discontents. Also, through being enrolled in a Brave Thinking Mastery class with Mary Morrisey as my mentor, I have gained the confidence to live the life I was designed for, to share my gifts to the world to make it a better place. The power within me, guided me every step of the way in writing this book.

You are reading this book because you want more. I am here to help you awaken your confidence in yourself that has always been there. With all these new tools, you will create new habits that will replace your old paradigms. You deserve more, and the power within you will guide you to more love, more relationships, better health, more money, better career and time, and money freedom.

God is greater than any circumstance; he wants you to live in joy and peace, have faith in him and he will see you safely through your own storms. You create your own storms, your own sickness and your own poverty. The will of God does not produce sickness, poverty, or pain; the will of God provides wholeness, abundance, and life in harmony with everyone.

"The greatest medicine of all, is teaching people they don't need medicine" . . . Hippocrates. It is your perception to believe that statement is true or false, both are right. It is where you put your power in believing. Same holds true for many things. It is your perception, you have full dominion over your perceptions and beliefs. If your life is not bringing you the right results, you need to change your perceptions and beliefs.

Your own fears stop you from living; your fear of sickness; your fear that no one loves you; your fear of poverty; your fear of what people think; your fear of old age; your fear of lack of freedom and your fear of death. Where your attention goes, energy flows. Cancel/delete any thoughts you don't want manifested into your life. Your life is a reflection of your thoughts. You are worrying so much, you never really live, up until now.

Your Spirit is internal and eternal; it never dies. Unfortunately, some of you never start living. Your spirit loves to be young and have fun. It's your thoughts, beliefs, and actions that make you get old. You think you have to act in a certain way to please others, or you think society expects you to act a certain way. I am not saying to act irresponsible, everyone is responsible for their own actions. I am saying be happy and youthful in your actions, please yourself. Your spirit will let you know if you are doing something wrong, you will feel not at ease. I remember, around 10 years ago, my mom asking me, "Diana, when are you going to grow up?" I responded, "never!" Why should I? Those words still hold true, I like being youthful and having fun, like Peter Pan. I don't want to grow old and neither does your spirit. Laughing is a great medicine. Try it!

The best way to help others is to help yourself; we all are connected as one. How you treat someone else will reflect back onto you. Be nice! Be the best that you can be at all times because karma could be a b**ch. When you smile or compliment someone, it is a good reflection back to you. When you are being nasty, talking behind peoples backs, talking down to others, or hurting someone's feelings, that is a negative reflection back to you. You will not achieve a good outcome from that. You are sending negative vibrations out and you will attract negative vibrations in, like a magnet. When you start to learn how to communicate with others in a more loving, positive way, you will see your life start unraveling in a more loving positive way. What you will sow is what you will reap. You can't plant apple seeds and expect oranges. You can't plant carrots and expect beets. Start planting seeds of what you want to grow in your life. In the game of life, there is no getting over on anyone. The Universe is always taking notes. You may think you can get over, but pay attention. Your negative actions will come back negatively in some form—through lack of money, poor relationships, your vocation (career), or poor health. Life is a give and take. Always give first. You want respect? Give respect. You want love? Give love. You want money? Give money. You want more time? Give more time to others. Don't ever say you don't have enough of any of them. That tightens the belt; you will struggle with all those. Everything is energy—keep positive energy flowing, and abundance in all areas will keep flowing.

Each of you is blessed with a gift or a talent that you are here to share. Sharing brings more manifestation. Dis/ease is a sure sign you are not sharing your gift or living your life purpose. You are blessed with one or more gifts to make life better and better. No one is left out. The only difference is some of you are more awake than others, and some are not awakened to this knowledge, up until now. There is no reason that at any age you can't start living. Age is a number and an excuse. If you keep up with your "Royal Flush," your kingdom will flourish. You will learn about this in chapters to follow.

Are you addicted to drama? If so, that is a sure sign you are not really living. You are so concerned how others are living. Spending hours watching TV, watching others live while you are sitting there fantasizing on a life you are envious of. Don't waste your energy on other people's drama; make your own. Become the life others are dreaming of. We are all children of God, and we all come here with the same amount of days in a year, the same 12 months in a year, the same seven days in a week, and the same 24 hours in a day—the only difference is how you are using your precious time. You can't get that time back. Don't dwell on the fact that you can't get your time back, you are wasting good energy on that thought. TV is a sure way to waste time and energy. It's ok in moderation; just don't make it your life. Facebook and other media outreaches are good in moderation also. You could touch other people's lives and make good connections. Don't overuse anything and waste your good energy. Your time is precious. I have a lot of energy because I know how to conserve my energy. I try not to waste it on things that are not productive, and draining. I always like to be in learning mode; if not, I like to inspire others and I have fun doing it. It's your life—design what you like and don't complain if life is not going your way. Today is the start of better days ahead, keep that focus. "I am getting better and better every day in every way!"

Life doesn't happen to you, and life doesn't happen for you—life happens through you, and it happens with you. God gave man dominion over the earth, and over the plants and the animals. He also gave you full dominion over your mind and your thoughts. You need to guard your mind, don't let anything in that you don't want. Choose proper surroundings and the environment you are in; it truly effects your whole well-being. If you can't change your surroundings and your environment right now, start visioning what you want, take whatever small action you could do, to change it up. Start with what you have, and you have much more than you know. Don't ever look at your conditions and accept them based on your circumstances. Your longing for more, should be your leader and guide—don't settle. Contentment is the enemy of success; it will stop you from seeking more and more. Your discontent should be your discovery for more. Claim what you want—good health, happiness, safety, prosperity, love, joy, peace, wisdom, friendships, truth, trust, and forgiveness. Keep these thoughts and keep saying these words to yourself daily. Your vibration will soon start attracting them into your life. The negative ones will move out. You will be amazed how energy works.

Are you successful? Highly successful people are willing to be uncomfortable to create more. They are always looking for opportunities to take action upon. They are always ready, even when it's not convenient. They keep a positive outlook that everything will all work out.

Are you a procrastinator? The "I'll do it tomorrow" person? You are always saying, "I'll do it tomorrow." Tomorrow never comes because it becomes today. You keep chasing tomorrow, always procrastinating. Waiting for things to get easier. Waiting for things to get better. Waiting for more money. Waiting for more ideas. Waiting for someone else to do it. You are always on the sidelines waiting.

Are you a failure? Unsuccessful people always have an excuse. You never have enough money. You never have enough time. You never have enough energy. You feel you're not loved. Unfortunately, you will never have anything, if you stay in the state of mind of having pity parties daily. "In any moment of decision, the best thing to do is the right thing; the next best thing is the wrong thing, but the worst thing to do is nothing" . . . Theodore Roosevelt. Get thinking! Get moving! Take a step, all the energy will start shifting. You don't need to know all the "hows", you just need to focus on "why" it's important, and everything will start shifting and maybe even rumbling. Come from the vision, change your feeling tone like it's already done.

Everything is a state of mind. You could be old at 30 and young at 90. You could be poor with $1,000,000.00, or you could be rich with $1000.00. You could feel loved with one partner, or you could feel lonely with 100 partners. It is all a state of mind. Henry Ford said, "If you think you can, you can . . . If you think you can't, you can't." Both are true.

Are you utilizing your six mental faculties that you were gifted at birth? Did you even know they existed? Or maybe you knew, but you don't use them to your best highest interest. You could go through life not opening your gifts and just accept what's going on. That would be a shame! I want to help you open your gifts that you were given. These gifts are all very important; they could work for you or against you—the ball is in your court. The gifts are Visualization, Imagination, Intuition, Will, Perception, and Persistence. Pay attention to see if you have unwrapped all your gifts, or maybe just a couple.

One of them is Visualization. How do you look at yourself and your world? You think in pictures, so if you want good things, you have to see them first. Are you seeing a tight, firm, sexy, young, healthy you? Or, do you see a fat, old, flabby, lazy, sickly you? Do you see a world of beautiful, loving, caring people around you? Or, do you see a world of hateful, harmful demons of destruction? The visual picture you keep in your mind magnetizes energy towards what you think of most. Start painting beautiful pictures in your mind. See yourself not as you are; see yourself as you want to be. See your world not as it is; see your world as you want it to be. See your children not as they are; see your children as you want them to be. See your spouse not as they are; see your spouse as you want him or her to be. See your job not as it is; see your job as you want it to be. See your finances not as they are; see your finances as you want them to be. See your living conditions not as they are; see your living conditions as you want them to be. See your physical things not as they are; see your physical things as you want them to be. See your health not as it is; see your health as you want it to be. Energy will start to shift in the direction of what you want. You have choices— if you don't have a vision, nothing moves. Keep the vision of what you want; don't put energy on anything you don't want. You create with vision. With learning this important gift, use it properly. God wants you to be happy along with all his children, it brings him joy, we are one with Infinite Intelligence. Keep the vision of heaven on earth, if everyone does it, we will create a more beautiful, peaceful world. Remember, keep the vision of what you want.

A fun one is Imagination. Children have great imaginations until their parents, teachers, or coaches shut down their images. Start being a child again— dream big, no limitations. Start seeing yourself in pictures, unlimited to your circumstances. Who are you? Who are you with? What are you driving?

Where are you living? What do your living quarters look like? What did you invent? How is your state of health? How many pounds do you weigh? How much money are you making? The sky is the limit! Now, really feel what it feels like. Try it on for size. How different would your life be? Does it feel good? It should feel wonderful! A bonus would be writing them down. I have a power page at the end of each chapter so you could write the answers of these questions down and anything else that you feel will amp up your power. An extra bonus would be making a vision board: cutting out pictures and putting them on a board so you could look at it daily. This action would give your vision a lot of energy. Speaking your vision out loud daily would amplify the power even more.

The next one is Intuition, which is also known as the sixth sense, your instinct. The five senses are seeing, hearing, smelling, tasting, and touching. Intuition is a knowing of truth and your instinctive behavior to a situation. You have a strong conviction, and you don't need scientific or physical results to prove your knowing. You just know. A peace and a calming feeling comes over you. It is the power within you confirming that. You don't need justification from others for your belief. Has anyone ever given you information and, right away, your insides jump out at you and say, "No way!" That happened to me when the doctor wanted to give me an operation to correct my lower back pain. My inner self refuted it, and I am so glad I listened. You'll hear about the story in a future chapter. When you have an important question, always quiet yourself, and connect to your higher self—it will guide you to the right choice. Sometimes that choice won't be the choice of the norm, but you have to learn to trust your instinct; it always knows best. Your instinct is your personal guide; it will never steer you wrong. Mine has always guided me since I was a young girl. It is a feeling of walking in faith, trust, and believing. It is something that needs to be practiced. You will get better and better at it over time, especially as you see the confirmations of the choices you were guided to pick.

The next one is Perception. I find this one to be very important. It could make or break you. How you perceive something is your perception. How do you see the glass? Half full or half empty? I see it refillable! Your perception is how you see things in life. If things aren't going well, you really need to change your perception on certain things. You should consider thinking positive and not just rely on your five senses to be your only truth and guide. Do you consider yourself a realist? If so, you create judgement from your 5 senses—seeing, touching, smelling, hearing, and tasting—and you need physical proof to bring you to your conclusion. You only look at physical proof and anything else is impossible. I hope this book could change your perception on your thoughts, especially if you are a realist. You don't live in a real world; you live in a metaphysical world. Things happen every day that you can't explain with physical proof. Infinite intelligence will make happen what you can't make happen. I can't help you to change your mindset, but you can. Everyone's perception is not the same; it is not always of truth, even if appears true in the physical. If someone says something to you that is very negative and you believe them, this will set a negative tone, and you will perceive it to be true. These negative words could be from a teacher, from a parent, from a coach, from a sibling, from a spouse, or from a doctor, and you may perceive them as speaking the truth—the truth is, it's up to you. The option is, you always have choice whether to accept what they say as truth or refute what they say. My advice is: don't accept anything you don't want as truth, unless you want it to be. You could perceive my advice as true or false; this will be your perception. Test your perception with your intuition; it will guide you. Like Henry Ford said, "If you think you can, you can . . . If you think you can't, you can't." It also holds true: if you think you're right, you're right . . . if you think you're wrong, you're wrong . . . if you think you're going to win, you'll win . . . if you think you're going to lose, you'll lose . . . if you think you're loved, you're loved . . . if you think everyone is against you, everyone is against you . . . if you think you're healthy, you're healthy . . . if you think you're dying, you're dying. Perception is very convincing when all odds are against you. This is when it will be in your best interest to change your perception. Start looking at things in a much more positive, assertive way. You don't live in a world depending on just your 5 senses—that's just in the physical. You live in a metaphysical world where anything is possible; it is best if you start perceiving this to achieve the results you want. You will need to amp up your Will and your Persistence to make these changes.

Your Will is what you truly want. This is your Heart's Desire—your longing for more and your Will to achieve it. When there is a Will, there is always a Way . . . All Things are Possible with God. Your Will is your powerhouse to believing this. You are thriving through your intuitive belief. All odds may seem to be against you, but your Will is your living testament and has the last say.

A large gift is Persistence. This is your drive. Persistence is you becoming unstoppable. A "Weeble" that never gets knocked down. "Weebles wobble, but they don't fall down." No matter how many times you get knocked down, you pop right back up. You are relentless. You become pin focused to the outcome. You are on a mission. Without a doubt, you will succeed with persistence. I have been told many times that I have a lot of persistence. I do feel like a "Weeble" at times. The power inside me is so much stronger than any circumstance around me. My will and my persistence have taken me through many challenges. I want you, to start using your same gifts that you have inside. You will conquer any challenge that comes your way; stay in faith.

What are the results that you have been getting up until now? I hope you're waking up! These small little changes will change the direction in which your life is going. Your thoughts are generating your feelings, and your feelings are generating your actions. In the next chapter, I will amp up the power of your thoughts and help guide you to create what you want in your life. It's your Life! It's in the palm of your thoughts.

"Change your Thoughts . . . Change your World."

POWER PAGE . . . AMP UP YOUR POWER!

(Write Your Thoughts, Words and Affirmations)

_____

_____

_____

_____

_____

_____

_____

_____

_____

_____

_____

_____

_____

_____

_____

_____

_____

_____

_____

_____

CHAPTER 2

THE POWER OF YOUR
THOUGHTS AND VISIONS

"As a man thinketh in his heart, so is he."
—Proverb 23:7

What are you constantly thinking about? Pay attention to your thoughts. Is your life reflecting your thoughts? Do you focus on your health, worrying about things that might happen? Do you focus on how you might not have enough money for your bills? Do you focus on loneliness? Do you focus on how you can't find a job? Do you ever think to yourself, "Oh wow, I was just thinking about that." What you focus upon is where you draw your energy towards. The more you think of what you don't want, it is creating a life of what you don't want around you. This creates more anxiety and depression because you're on a never ending mouse wheel, going around in circles and never creating the life you do want. I want you to get off the wheel of sameness and get on the yellow brick road to a life of happiness created and by designed by you. Let's pave the way!

First, stop having your pity parties! Why me? Let me answer your question. Why not you? Magnetize what you want. When a thought comes creeping in of something you don't want, hit the delete button. Your mind is similar to a computer; you are connected to the infinite, just like the internet. You are born with so much knowledge already inside of you. Society makes you think that you have no knowledge, that you are born stupid; you are definitely not stupid. God doesn't create junk. You have all the knowledge inside you waiting to be tapped into, like a computer. You are connected to intelligence. No one is left out because of their color, religion, or poverty. These are very poor, damaging, limiting beliefs and paradigms that have been passed on through the centuries. It is just a lack of belief, a lack of thinking, and a lack of knowing. Thinking is the most underused source of energy. It is a terrible thing to waste. We need to get more people thinking, instead of brain washing false knowledge in. You need to get the knowledge out, using the infinite knowledge within. You have many gifts and talents within you, you could be master of all. Take me for instance, I don't think there was a time in my life that I wasn't doing at least 3 things at once. I am always working on different skills, I love to stay busy. I don't know what the word bored feels like. My personal rule is: I strive to live a life of everything I love doing and be around the people I love being around. I am a sponge for learning more and more, and I love becoming more and more. It brings me more life to bring that feeling tone to you, so you may experience a life that you would enjoy living, instead of just accepting a life by default.

Your soul purpose is to be better than the generation before you. You are here to create a heaven on earth, not to carry on the negative defects of disease, addictions, or poverty from your past generations. It's not your genes that control you; it's the environment and your beliefs. Refute what you don't want! It's your purpose to change up the negative thoughts and beliefs that have been carried down through the many generations. Break the chains. Cut the heavy baggage that you have been dragging around. Do not accept that you are going to have a disease, an addiction, or poverty, just because your ancestors did. It's not in your DNA, unless you believe it is. You have the power to refute what you don't want by pin focusing on what you do want. I stress upon pin focus. Don't let your fears, doubts, or worries pull you into "stinkin thinkin." It's a poison to your whole being; it could put you in a state of "dis/ease" if you don't do something about it. You may think and believe, "This is how it is, and I need to accept it." That is Bull Crap!!! Say, "No, Thank You!" to what you don't want—Cancel/Delete those thoughts and don't keep looking back. *"Each day is a new baby day!"* . . . Mary Morrissey.

God wants you to live a life of abundance, full of great health, free from pain, with lots of laughs and happiness, loving relationships with family and friends, a loving spouse, and a career that you love, while using your talents and your gifts to make this planet a better place than how you found it. You can't take anything with you when you leave, but you could surely leave a legacy behind, that will impact many generations to come after you. Life is forever evolving, getting better and more expansive, with more and more new technology. We are not meant to stay stagnant; our thoughts need to search for more and more. Never feel like you have to settle. This is where *dis/ease* happens—when your body is not at ease with the thoughts. Thoughts saying one thing and the body another. Your body needs to start listening to your thoughts and become one with your spirit. It's a mind, body, spirit connection. Your spirit is the master that gets shut down or put to sleep when your mind and body are not connecting. Don't let the body dictate to the mind all about its pain, suffering, and lack. Let the mind and thoughts control the body and give all pain, suffering, addictions, and poverty to the spirit. Spirit will guide you to your best highest interest. There is no pain, no suffering, no addictions, and no poverty when you are one with your spirit. Walk in complete faith, and spirit will guide you.

Negative thoughts are never working for your benefit. Cancel/delete the thought: "think of the worst, hope for the best." That is not a good way to use your energy. Instead, "Think of the best, and expect only the best," is a higher vibration of words and brings a higher vibration of results. Worries, doubts, and fears block your blessings. There was a story I once heard that sticks in my mind, and I believe it helped me see things in a new perceptive: The devil was teaching his little nephews how to take over the souls of people. He said, "The easiest way is through doubts, worries, and fears; they are always thinking these thoughts, and it will allow us to get in to block their blessings." When I really started thinking about it, it does make a lot of sense. I really started paying even more attention, to my thoughts, feelings, and doubts. I always walked with faith; now I run with faith! I don't want any of my blessings being blocked, and I am sure you don't either.

Another big thing that blocks your blessings is the act of not forgiving; it burdens you and causes dis/ease in your whole body. Forgive those that may have hurt you, cheated on you, deceived you, talked about you, or swindled you. Release and send them blessings of love and prayers that they may find the light. When you perform a forgiveness in your mind, and you release them from your soul, it benefits you more than them. Keep that practice of forgiveness nightly, as you are saying your gratitude prayers. Forgive those that bothered you during the day, don't hold on to negative vibrations, they burden you. Release the junk from your trunk, every night, for a peaceful sleep. You will notice, as you become more and more empowered, you will attract less junk, less confrontations, and become more and more at peace.

You are trained to think using your five senses — seeing, hearing, smelling, touching, and tasting — they give you the physical answers in life. It seems only normal to depend on them, because you were taught that "seeing is believing." It should only make sense to think that way. I am here to tell you, there is so much more than that. Your 5 senses are in the physical, but we live in a metaphysical world. If you only live in the physical, you are only limited to the physical, your body, your mind and your beliefs, don't go beyond that. When you open your mind, and stop living in a box, you expand your awareness, there is so much more, and your life becomes so much more. There is an infinite connection of source, when you live in the spirit, using your creative thinking.

Every one of your thoughts are energy. Stop wasting energy on meaningless thoughts. You were born to be a creator, to use your life energy, to create more and more and better and better. Everything is created twice—first in the mind and then in substance. It is like your thoughts are being poured into a mold when you keep your thoughts pinned and focused on it. One of my greatest tools that I have learned to sharpen is being a *visionary*. I started using vision to create the life I wanted from a very young age. I didn't think anything of it; I just *visioned* and I always stayed in gratitude. At a young age, I visioned getting married young to a wonderful, handsome man who would show me lots of love and respect, want children, is handy like my dad, and likes to have fun and share a beautiful home together. As of today, 36 years later, I have to say my angels did a great job helping me fill that order. The one big challenge I've had to deal with regarding my soul mate, is teaching him how to speak to others, and myself, when he would get twisted. He had somewhat of a rude Brooklyn attitude when he didn't get his way . . . lol. I'll speak more about that in the chapter, "Words have Power."

I truly used my thoughts to create, and I didn't even know that I was doing it. I was always a visionary, and you will see how it became an asset. Christmas, 1984, Den asked me to marry him. The beautiful engagement ring was dangling on the Christmas tree and, of course, I said yes. We planned a wedding for May 17, 1986. My parents had told us they were going to pay for the wedding, which was an old-fashioned tradition. We were thrilled and grateful. I thought, "What's the next step? We need a home to live in." Pay attention to your wants and longings. We both had some money saved and I ideally wanted a home before we got married. We decided on living in Brooklyn. That is where Den and his brother had an auto body shop. I wanted a detached home; since I was used to living in Long Island and that's how most of the homes were, that's what I envisioned living in. We went to a realtor and we described what we wanted. One of the first homes she took us to was detached. It was in Canarsie, about 2 miles away from Den's shop. It was the messiest house on the block, inside and out, so, of course, we wanted to see more. We looked for over a month, one worse than the other, not fitting our needs, and not detached. I kept thinking of the first home and started visioning it all done and walking to the park with my future children and my husband being nearby. We put in a bid and got it. We closed on it in June, almost a year before the wedding. We started renovations, and it was like dominos—one thing after another needed to get done. By the time the wedding came, we had our kitchen and bedroom done, two important things that we absolutely wanted done. I envisioned having a really nice honeymoon; I became a travel agent so I could book what I wanted at a discounted rate. I booked a really nice, 14-day honeymoon in Hawaii. A week on two of the islands and a week cruising around to all the islands. I saved a lot of money, and we were treated like royalty because I was an agent. Everything was so great, except I got sea sick. I didn't vision that . . . lol. The honeymoon was well thought out and deserved after all the house and wedding planning. I don't tell you these things to impress you; I tell you stories to impress upon you that you could create a life that you want. You don't have to live a life by default, that you are settling for. Things are surely not always going to be as perfect as you planned; there are always bumps in the road. The thing is, don't get discouraged in continuing to think and create. Some people, spend more time planning a vacation, than they do designing a life they want to live, is that you? Work with a coach to help you break the patterns that keep bringing you the same results. Nothing changes unless your thoughts, words and actions start shifting towards the positive.

Everything you create needs a blueprint. Work with what you have, you don't need to know all the hows, take a step, keep visioning, take another step, and another, and another. When a baby tries to walk, then falls down, the baby doesn't give up—it gets right back up and tries again. You have to go through a variety of steps, maybe even a few bumps and bruises. Get up, brush yourself off, and take another step. Some things come easier than others. Persistence is the name of the game. You have to really want it and work hard for your vision. Keep gratitude in your attitude, every step of the way. Do everything with a loving pleasure. Watch how things manifest. Keep vibrating positive thoughts of your vision. Come from your vision. Keep a vision tone that it is already accomplished.

Continuing with my visioning in Canarsie, we ended up having three healthy children, and I used to walk to the park with them, all the time. Den loved the short drive to work. All the renovations in the home got done; it took about 10 years to complete everything. I loved how everything turned out, and we thought, "Ok, this is great, what's next?" We had friends moving to Staten Island so we decided maybe it was time for us to move also. Remember, your inner self is always expanding for more. We both decided we were not going to renovate another home; we decided it would be easier to design it and get someone to build it. So, that is exactly what happened. We found a nice piece of property on a nice cul-de-sac, where a builder was offering to build any designed home with a set of plans. That was great and pretty amazing. Being a realtor now for the last 13 years, I know it is not that often that a builder will build something other than what they planned for, but, remember, it was my vision, so anything was possible. I had an architect draw up plans from my vision. My husband gave me full control; he figured *happy wife, happy life*. The truth was he didn't want to be bothered thinking about all the fine details. There were a lot of details to think about, but I didn't mind.

God says the same thing to you: design me a life you want. You might just say: design me a nice life. You may be feeling how my husband felt. You don't want to think about all the fine details that you want in your life, so you will leave it up to God. You might be living a life of default, and just take each day as it comes. That is fine if you're content, you're not meant to be just content, your spirit is always seeking for more. If there is an area in your life, that you're not really happy with, tell the Architect (God) to make some changes. I had to go to my house architect a few times before he got my vision down right. So, the same goes with your vision. Make sure it's what you really want; try it on for size. I used to have to vision how I would feel in each room of my home. The architect would say, "I don't think you will like stepping down into your family room and having a step down to your living room." I would have to say, "Yes, I would, and please design it that way." Another thing he would say, "You're making the closets too big." I would say, "I want big closets," and trust me, I filled them up . . . lol. The architect finally gave me everything I asked for; it took about 2 years to build, but I have no regrets.

I loved the design and loved how it all came out, it was even better than I visioned. God always, over delivers your expectations, when you stay in faith. We had to have a lot of patience. Originally the builder said it would take 6 months; it ended up taking 2 years. That is another thing with visions and your life; it's not always going to go as fast as you like, but trust the process and learn to go with the flow. It's on God's time. Don't get frustrated! The affirmation that I kept saying was, "All good things come to those who wait." I think those words might have delayed it a bit, but it was a nice journey, with a lot of bumps in the road. The thing to remember: I never turned on the fear, doubt, or worry switch. Many times, my husband did; he would start with the negative crap, but I would have to cancel/delete those thoughts really quickly.

The truth is, you have to walk in faith. God always has your back. Remember, thoughts are either giving you power, or thoughts are taking power away. What are you thinking?

The worst thing to do is nothing, second worst is not believing you are worthy of receiving. You may have been given great opportunities, gifts, wonderful people in your life, great health, a recovery from a disease, a recovery from an addiction, or you may have gotten ahead financially, you have a great job, you have a great partner, *but*, all of a sudden, you start thinking, "What if . . . ???" I want to say that this is one of your biggest downfalls. With a blink of an eye everything could start tumbling, if that is where you keep your thoughts. When life starts really getting good, stay grateful. When you start doubting the process—losing faith, doubting people in your life, worrying that a disease or addiction will come back, worrying about money, worrying about keeping a certain job, worrying about your partner cheating on you, worrying someone is better than you—this becomes an invitation for the downfall. This is very important to work on, and it is key, that you don't put worries, doubts, or fears in your thoughts. Too many people have challenges with this.

My huge thought, which became more powerful while writing this book, is to have many Inspirational centers, helping to Awakening the Power within. Starting with the one on Staten Island. Having life coaching, inspiring and awakening people's faith within themselves. When you don't have support, paradigms pull you to fears, doubts and worries. The enemy takes over. A coach, like in any sport, helps keep you focused on getting better at your game. The game I am writing about in this book, is the Game of Life, and all the pieces that are needed. You need support and guidance in playing the Game of Life. There are Universal laws to be followed, that you may not know about. I feel there should be ministries spreading the word to everyone. God's laws. You also need a partner in believing in your dreams; with God all things are possible. People need to connect to God, the Infinite Power, breathing you. You were gifted with a purpose. What brings you life? I feel bringing this question to you, is mine.

God created the Universe and this beautiful planet that we live on. His thinking is of a superior intelligence. Everything is so precise and works like clock work. Nature is so amazing. Take time to look around and see all the natural wonders. It is said, "God created you in his like image"—perfect. Knowing this, the same intelligence that is in "Him" is in you. God even went as far as to send Jesus, to teach you, your power within is as great as his. He quoted it many times in the bible. I am not here to preach about religion; I am here to share a message from the spirit that is within you. Many of you don't believe and understand it, yet. Keep an open mind. The message is, "The same Power that was in Jesus is the same Power that is within you." I know this is a powerful statement. It is a powerful message that God wants me to bring forth to you. You may not want to turn water into wine or walk across the water, but if you have a burning desire to do something, overcome something, invent something, or accomplish something, the power is within you. On the physical, you don't need to know all the *hows*; your spirit just needs to know the *why*, if it has good in it for others, it will be accomplished. It has to be a powerful *why* that will benefit others. Golden Rules to follow: Go through life as you are one; "Love thyself;" "Love thy neighbors;" "Don't do to others, what you would not like done to you." In other words, "Do unto others as you would like done unto you."

So, I was able to design a great husband that I wanted, three healthy children, and a nice home, twice. You might say that is just a coincidence, and I'm just lucky. Everything seemed great until I brought upon myself some health issues. Maybe building the house was stressful, but I never let it show, and I never knew how much it affected my body. Our home was complete in June 1997. In the year 2000, at age 37, I was diagnosed with Grade IV Spondylothesis; I had arthritis, severe low back pain, sciatica, and limited movements, before feeling a lot of pain. I couldn't even stand long in one position, without feeling pain. My lower back had a big knot; it felt like a ball of fire. I used to get out of bed feeling like a 90 year old woman and thinking, "I can't have this; I am way too young to be feeling like this." I had gone to an orthopedic doctor to have x-rays to check everything out. The diagnoses was not good. The doctor wanted to give me cortisone shots and pain killers, both of which I didn't accept. The doctor then gave me a prognosis. He said, "If you don't get an operation to put a pin in your lower back, you will end up in a wheel chair." I remember thinking to myself and having this little conversation: "Back operations don't work, I know so many people that had them and are still in pain and on meds." (my inner voice) I refuted what he said, in my thoughts, and I just kept picturing myself healed. He also told me not to exercise because it would make it worse. I also refuted accepting that. I kept thinking the exercise is going to get me better and better. I kept refusing any shots for pain and any pills. My inner self said, "None of that." I kept thinking my body was going to heal better without them. I was quite stubborn about taking meds (I personally feel meds are a band-aid). I never gave meds power, so that continued to be my belief. By not giving meds a power, I had to find a stronger power. I found that stronger power within myself. Remember, your belief controls your life. If you are on any meds, and you believe they are working, that is the power of your thoughts, God bless, stick to what works for you.

Another message I have to bring to you is: "Don't let any circumstances of addiction to any substances, be bigger than the power within you." When you put power on a negative symptom, or substance, that you feel has control over you, you make it bigger, and your power smaller. You are diminishing all your God-given powers and allowing something else to have control. Take full dominion over your thoughts. Remember, "The Power Within You . . . is Greater than any Circumstance around you!" What do you truly want? What thoughts are you trying to numb? Cancel/ Delete the negative thoughts, go to a different program. Work with life coach or a holistic minister. Don't carry unwanted baggage. Every day is a new beginning. A bad chapter is not your whole book. Each day you start with a clean page. What would you like to read, in the story of your life? A good lesson would be to write a couple of chapters on a life you would love living. Jot down on the power page at the end of the chapter what you would love your life to look like in three years. Start living from that dream. Send out the vibration.

It is your Will to accept something or refute it. Stay guarded to what gets into your mind. Don't allow negative naysayers to take away your power and your belief. A diagnosis or a prognosis is just a symptom that your body is *not at ease;* it is not functioning at neutral; it is not at peace. A prescribed pill, a drug, or alcohol to numb the pain, is not the answer. Even, at times, an operation is not always the answer, as it wasn't for me. I felt I needed to get to the root of my health issues. I gritted through my pain, and I kept the vision of what I wanted and kept asking my Infinite Intelligence within me, to guide me, and it did. "Ask and Your Spirit will help." I taught myself Pilates and Yoga, and I attended some classes, always gritting through the pain with the knowing, and the faith, I was getting better and better every day. I didn't have one doubt in my mind. It took about 6 months of working on it almost every day. I was seeing a couple of different chiropractors; it was too painful for typical adjustments, so they used the EMS (Electric Magnetic Sensory), which are energy pulses, which I do believe in, because we are energy. One of the chiropractors took X-rays; she knew my diagnoses and saw the results. She said, "You are not going to believe this, you had a miracle; your body built a bridge where there was a separation." With all the work I was doing, and with my thoughts and words, my pain soon diminished, I continued getting better and better. Around the same time after the other diagnoses, I was told I had pre-cancerous cells in my cervix. That put a little fear into me, but I refuted the fear, and I wanted to learn more on how to get well. I wanted answers, and I didn't like the answers I was given. This was a big wake up call for me. I felt I needed to soak up more knowledge so I could share it. So, I was drawn to the College of Natural Medicine, and I studied as a Holistic Health Practitioner for Two years. They were shut down for some strange reason, so I had to take my credits to another Holistic University. I did a lot more studying, and I achieved many certifications in different areas. I became a Dream Builder coach, three years ago, through Mary Morrisey, Life Soulutions. I became a nutrition and wellness coach through Dr. Sears and, two years ago, I was led to become a Minister Practitioner, my spirit guiding me every step of the way. Now, after more than 16 years in the field of wellness, I need to share how to awaken the power within you, so you can start healing from the inside. Awaken!

Let's have you start thinking and working with a couple of challenges in your life. Get a piece of paper, or write alongside the question, also get a pencil, so you can make changes. Thoughts are like a slippery fish—if you don't write them down, they will slip away. Let's awaken your thinking power. Answer these questions, honestly:

Are you thinking the same thoughts you thought yesterday?

What are you mostly thinking about?

Do you keep your thoughts limited to your circumstances?

Do you keep your thoughts limited to how much money you have in the bank?

What are your thoughts, about money?

Do you respect money?

Do you love money?

What is the ideal amount of money you would want to be making monthly?

Do you love yourself?

How do you vision the best version of yourself?

Do you love people?

Do you have friends?

Are you in a loving relationship?

Do you want to be in a loving relationship?

Do you love your family?

Do you love work?

Do you love the time you spend alone?

What is it that you are seeking?

What would give you life?

Where would you like to take a vacation?

What would the ideal career be for you?

What is your ideal weight?

What are your ideal living conditions?

What is your ideal car?

What would your ideal partner be like?

What would your ideal family be like?

What would your ideal self be like?

What do you feel is your best quality?

What are your talents?

The questions could go on and on; give yourself an interview. You will really start learning about yourself. Start to really think about what you want. Start to get to know, You! As you notice your wants, you'll notice what you don't want. I don't want you to put any energy into what you don't want. Hit the cancel/ delete button when you notice it happening. Think about love, health, happiness and prosperity when a negative thought tries to move in. When you fill your thoughts with positive energy, the negative thoughts can't move in.

To awaken, you need to start dreaming. Start by daydreaming, something that you may have been told to stop doing. Pretend someone gave you a magic wand, and they asked, "What is the life you want to live?" Start by envisioning the life you want to live. Try to be very, very specific and detailed. Now try it on for size. Feel it in your mind. It may look good, but how will all the circumstances feel after it is complete? Are you having any more longings or discontents? Now, once you have thought the vision, write it down, and say the vision. See and hear the vision, again try it on. It is very important to be very specific with your thoughts. Be in the dream and notice the fine details—the more specific the better. Now, you have to come from that dream, and it's like you have to create a bridge to it. So, from where you are now, what is the next step you could take to get you closer to your dream or your vision? Make a list of different options. Try doing a few of the options and you will be on your way. Once you change your energy patterns, things start to shift, towards your vision.

Pack up fears, doubts, and worries, and send them on their way; they are not welcome to take up any occupancy, in your mind. Put out the "No Vacancy" sign for any negative stuff.

I want you to move Love, Joy, Faith, Peace, Wisdom, Health, Happiness, Prosperity, Truth, Friendships, Trust, Forgiveness, and Safety, all into your mind, body, and soul. Into every trillion of your cells, taking up all the vacancy of your mind, body and soul. Fill your self with this feeling tone; how do you feel? You should feel amazing and at peace.

Now that you have mastered and amped up the Power of your Thinking, lets go onto the next chapter to master and amp up the *Power of your Words.*

POWER PAGE . . . AMP UP YOUR POWER!

(Write Your Thoughts, Words and Affirmations)

_____

_____

_____

_____

_____

_____

_____

_____

_____

_____

_____

_____

_____

_____

_____

_____

_____

_____

_____

_____

_____

_____

CHAPTER 3

THE POWER OF YOUR WORDS AND SOUNDS

Words hold a lot of Power. They hold a vibration. The statement, "Sticks and Stones may break my bones, but words will never hurt me," is so far from the truth. Your tongue is like a sword.

Words have energy inside them, negative ones do hurt, and they stick with you for a long time. Words could bring you up or tear you down if you are not careful with them. When someone is talking down to you or telling you something you don't want to accept, refute what they are saying. Cancel/delete the words before they get in. Words could do a lot of harm, but could also do a lot of great things. It depends on how you use your words. I really suggest you start paying attention to every word that you say. Up until now, your life has been a reflection of them. Don't let the words get inside you. *"All the water on the earth cannot drown you, unless it gets inside you"* . . . Eleanor Roosevelt. *"Stand guard at the portal of your mind"* . . . Ralph Waldo Emerson. I have to give credit to Mary Morrissey for teaching me these two powerful statements, which are great tools. Both of the statements have the same message: you have control of what you let in; become a master protector; only let in what you want to let in—you are in control.

You are where you are, because of the words you let in and the words you let out. Words become your destiny. The statement, "You're going to eat those words," has been said throughout the centuries. Words are like seeds—what you toss out there, you will sow. Be prepared to eat the fruit or the poison of what you put out there. Plant the seeds of only what you want to eat. If you plant right, the seeds will grow into a beautiful garden. What you plant today is what you will reap tomorrow.

Don't verbalize what you don't want. My husband used to do it all the time. I still catch him saying negative things here and there. I cancel/delete them, if I hear them. He would tell me everything that could go wrong with all different things, then when it happened, he would say, "See, I'm the wizard." I would laugh at him and shake my head. I would always say, "No, you are creating it." He would get so mad, when I would say that. Of course, he didn't believe me, or want to hear me say that. When he would complain to me about his workers at his shop, I would say, "Stop saying negative things about them. If you want positive results, start saying good things, and vision them doing great work." Again, he didn't realize the atmosphere he was creating. I told him to start praising their work. Start visioning how you want your shop to run. Visualize it running smoothly with the best, talented workers. My husband is a work in progress, and he sees that I do make a lot of sense. Worries, doubts, and fears block your blessings; I choose to walk in faith, trust, and confidence, and I get better results. I can't change any of my loved ones; I can only help guide them to make the changes themselves—the same thing goes for you, the words you choose are your choice. No one can change your life for you, except you.

Never speak or put any energy on words that you don't want in your life. Retract and start creating a life that you do want, with your words. I want great health, happiness, safety, and prosperity for my family and myself. I want a happy, loving, fun marriage. I want a fun, meaningful career that never feels like work. I want to go on family vacations with my whole family and friends. I want to travel, see the world, and make a difference while doing it. I want to keep creating more and more. I love my life and I am grateful for it.

Make a list of your wants, try them on for size, say them out loud, you could borrow some of mine, change them up if you have to, and then own them. Say it like it already is. Plant them in your mind and watch them grow. You must think of your seeds as fragile seedlings—don't tell too many naysayers about your vision; you don't want their poisoning words to hurt the process. Water your seeds daily with loving, caring, and grateful thoughts. You might ask, "Why do I need to be grateful for something I didn't receive yet?" The answer is: I don't really know why, I just know it is the fuel for receiving. I guess the Universe (God) just likes to hear the words, "Thank you." I know I like to hear those words. I notice that when people are grateful, for the little things I do for them, I like to do more for them. The same thing goes for when people just keep complaining and just want more and more, and never say thank you. I know for myself, I don't like to do anything for them, because I don't feel appreciated. Who would want to serve an ungrateful person? God has feelings also. You are his child. He wants you to be a reflection of his love to the world, through your words, and through your actions. He wants you to awaken and enjoy the gifts he has giving you. Say, "Thank you!"

What type of person are you? Do you blurt out negative things all day long about yourself and others? Or do you pay attention to the words coming out of your mouth? Do you use curse words? Stop it! You are cursing yourself, when you say them. They have a very low vibration. You will attract low vibrational occurrences. Like attracts like. Low vibrational words attract low vibrational results.

I learned at a very early age that words hurt, and cause harm to others. When I was in 3rd or 4th grade, I remember girls at my table were making fun of a girl who had greasy hair. They were calling her dirty. I didn't do anything to stop it, so I was just as guilty. The next day, she didn't come to school. I remember her mom coming up to school and telling me how sick her daughter was; she was throwing up, because of what was said to her. That made me feel sad, and really bad. I knew that I would never want to be part of making anyone feel bad again. It really hurt me inside. When you hurt others, you hurt yourself, one way or another. When my children were in school, I was very involved with the PTA and the Leadership team. I was a big advocator of the non-bullying programs. It is a serious concern, and it should not be taken lightly. Children need to learn, at an early age, how powerful words are. They also need to learn how to protect themselves from words getting in. Words can be carried on for decades, if you don't know how to release them. Try working with energy healers, Reiki masters, as they can help you release some blockages. Words create many blockages. We are energy, and need to keep everything flowing; if not we create dis/ease within ourselves.

Try using more loving, caring words. High vibrational words will attract high vibrational results. It's not about luck; it is about your thoughts, words, and actions. They all create a vibration. When you are in tune with a high vibration, you will feel, when people are speaking in a negative vibration near you. Try to have talks with people with a high vibration, a positive attitude, you will connect better and feel better. They are usually people with a smile on their face.

We live in a metaphysical world, unfortunately, your subconscious doesn't know right from wrong. Your subconscious is your genie in a lamp—it hears and listens to what you are constantly saying and aims to give you what you want by what you say. You end up creating a life that you really don't want, because of the words you are constantly saying. Start paying attention. *"Say what you want, really want what you say."* Claim what you want. Claim them as you drift off to sleep.

Words have an impact on people. There is a certain energy when you put some of the words together. Alone, they may not have an impact, but when you sew them together, they build a bridge of faith. Take notice of all the great quotes and statements. Inspirational quotes help you through the day. They have so much power and meaning behind them. There have been many great people that have made an impact with their words. We like to give credit to those who have made great statements or have used words in certain phrases. They are all God's words, especially words of truth and divinity, and are meant to be shared by everyone, for everyone. I have used these words to help me get better: "I Am Getting Better and Better Every Day in Every Way." I said these powerful words everyday when I was trying to get better from my stage 4 Spondolythesis. I gritted through my pain and the words helped me through. Between my thoughts, words, and actions, I did heal, and I am pain free. I still use those words daily. Those words have power, and they are for everyone to share. I hope they will make a difference for you in your life.

What do you want in your life? Pretend I have a tape recorder. Think it out first. Really think. Now really tell me what you want. Don't tell me what you want from the circumstances you are living in right now. Tell me what you want. Focus. Describe in words the life you want. Be very specific. The Law of Specificity is very crucial. First, visualize it. Feel how it feels. Try it on for size. Does it feel expensive and life giving, or does it feel constrictive and uncomfortable? Words you think and say, start to take form in the Universe, it is really necessary to *say what you want and really want what you say, I can't stress that enough. Trust me; it is for your great benefit.*

Some words have more power than others. I have found that "I am" is very powerful; you should use these words very wisely. I actually cringe when I hear people not using the words correctly. I feel the need to correct you, when I hear you using, "I am" in a way that is not in your best interest. "I am" is like saying "God Is." "I am" is very powerful, so never say anything after those two words that you don't want to claim into your life. Your conscious hears it and knows for sure, you don't want the negative verbs and adverbs that that you are saying, like: I am fat, I am old, I am sick, I am disabled, I am ugly, I am too slow, I am lonely, I am tired, I am an addict, I am broke, I am a gambler, I am an alcoholic, I am a loser, I am poor, I am stupid, I am disorganized, I am always late, I am a procrastinator . . . and the list goes on and on. Cancel/ Delete! Your subconscious doesn't know the difference between the positive or negative verbs. Think of your subconscious as a commuter. If you keep typing in "I am fat, I am tired, I am lonely," what results do you think you are going to get? All the negative things you have been typing in take form in your life, sooner or later. Up until now. Your computer follows your command, as if you are claiming something you want. If it hears it enough times over and over, it will create what you don't want. Your subconscious is your Genie in a bottle. Your wish is its command. So, really pay attention and pick and choose your words very carefully after the words "I Am." A better choice of words would be: I am amazing, I am at a perfect body weight of . . . (claim a # that would feel right), I am beautiful, I am perfect in Gods image, I am energized, I am lovable, I am caring, I am an overcomer, I am healed, I am happy, I am healthy, I am intelligent, I am a millionaire, I am full of wisdom, I am organized, I am prosperous, I am loving, I am successful and I am sexy! Claim what you want. Say all these "I ams" in confidence. At first, some may not feel right in the conscious (physical) because the conscious might not believe it at first, but soon your subconscious (your genie in a bottle) will manifest it for you—they are all great qualities to own up to. Remember, God created you, and he does not create junk—you are perfect in his image.

Another powerful two words: "I have." And that is like saying "God has," and many use it to say they have some sort of dis/ease. "I have" is making a claim to something. You are owning up to it. When you make a claim that you have something, make sure it is something that you really want to own. I suggest highly that you refute claiming what you don't want. It may appear real in the physical, and you may have all the physical symptoms and conditions, but don't give the words energy in the spiritual realm. Never own up to something you don't want, even if all odds seem to line up against you. Instead of saying, "I have an auto-immune disease, I have cancer, I have an addiction, I have a disability, I have no friends, I have no money, I have no one that loves me, I have a mental disability, I have an attention disorder, I have a phobia, I have an allergy, I have sex issues, I have learning issues," refute saying these things— ever. Cancel/Delete! Don't own up to them, unless, you want them, to move into your life. Don't unpack these bags. They might be uninvited guests for now, but soon you will conquer that challenge. If it is a dis/ease, say whichever applies: I have a challenge with . . . (whatever dis/ease); I have a challenge with . . . (whatever addiction); I have a challenge with money; I have a challenge with eating; I have a challenge with learning; I have a challenge with love; I have a challenge with making friends; I have a challenge with relationships; I have a challenge keeping a job; I have a challenge at work; I have a challenge with working; I have a challenge with exercising; I have a challenge with walking; I have a challenge with hearing; I have a challenge with tasting; I have a challenge with seeing; I have a challenge with speaking; I have a challenge with running; etc. A challenge is looked at by the subconscious as something that could be fixed. The spirit loves challenges; nothing is to big or to small for the spirit to overcome. You must believe this with conviction.

Never say you can't do something. "Can't" shuts you down; don't even say it jokingly. By changing your words, you are letting your subconscious know you are not owning or claiming what someone may have told you. The word "can't" is claiming defeat, spirit doesn't want that, you're shutting spirit down. When you say, "I could," your life spirit starts working on the "how to fix it." You don't need to worry about *how* it will get done. Focus your energy on the *why* you want it done. The *why* has to be powerful, and a soul desire. Challenges, issues, and problems are meant to be fixed and dealt with. When you say "I have . . ." it takes on ownership and settles comfortably in. Your new affirmation and claim is, "I have the Power to refute anything I don't want . . . I am ready for the Challenge . . . it will soon be under my feet . . . I am an Overcomer . . . Amen!"

Amen is a powerful word—it means sealed with God!

"I will" is also very powerful. It is like saying "God will," so, again, make sure any words after "I will" are positive. Never say: I will fail; I will lose; I will get sick. Cancel/Delete! No negative words! Instead, say: I will succeed! I will ace the test! I will achieve my goals! Get the picture? No more negative words! Don't ever verbalize, what you don't want. Repeat: "I will create, a great habit, of only saying, what I want, and really, wanting what I say!"

How do you start your morning? Get in the habit of saying, "Good Morning . . . (your name); I Love You," give yourself a big smile! These three little things, could make a huge difference, on how the rest of your day goes. Each one of your cells will have a positive, powerful reaction to those words and actions. Try it!

When you're in the shower, or getting ready, say some positive affirmations; especially ones that you may have challenges with . . . I am happy; I am blessed; I am tight, firm, and sexy; I am healthy; I am prosperous; I am successful; I am intelligent; I am organized; I am always on time; etc. Like the saying goes, "Fake it till you make it," especially with your words. Create a confidence of knowing it is already done. You are a reflection of your words; choose very wisely. Keep saying positive affirmations, reflecting the person you want to be or become. Words are a great reinforcement and a great way to push out any lingering negative thoughts. When you fill your mind with positive words, the negative thoughts have to move out. There is absolutely no vacancy for anything negative. Only create vacancy, for positive words, and positive thoughts.

Choose words that are life giving. As you start changing your words, you start changing your life and the lives around you. Say only good things about your family, friends, co-workers, government, and world. Like the saying goes, "If you don't have anything good to say, don't say it." That statement is very powerful and holds truth behind it. Each word holds energy and amplifies as it goes out into the infinite. This is why negative things are happening throughout the world. Too many negativists. Negative words attract negative actions. This is a very important, crucial message. It should not be taken lightly. You have the power to be part of the change in the world that you want to see. By sending out higher vibrational words and thoughts, you could be a part of world peace. What is going on today on our planet is a reflection of everyone's thoughts and words from yesterday. You are reaping the seeds you planted. Don't post negative things on social media—you are sending out more negative vibrations. Be the change you want to see in the world— post happy, inspiring posts to cheer people up. When you start changing your thoughts, words, and actions, the world around you will change. Let's focus on the good of our Earth. The Earth is abundant and always seeking more and more. The Earth has an endless supply of filling all its needs. The Earth is always expanding, forward and upward, to better and better. If you use negative words about your earth, you are causing more harm than good. Don't focus on lack—you will create more lack. Turn that channel or cancel/delete all those negative words that you are putting out there. You could do your own part to create a heaven on earth, choose positive words, when speaking about anyone, and your planet. I thank you in advance for helping.

Let's clean out the trash, and give Mother Earth some respect.

Something else to be concerned about is how you speak to others. How are you coming across to others and your loved ones? What is your tone? What is the attitude of what you are saying? Practice managing your voice and take notice of how you sound. Take note of the pitch of your voice. A higher pitched voice could sound like you are whining, and a lower pitched voice, could sound like you are bullying. When answering a question with a high pitch, it sounds doubting. How quickly are you speaking? Be mindful of your pace. People can't understand you, if you are rambling on. Don't go too slow; that could be taken as, demeaning and offensive. Be careful on the volume. Yelling, will only cause another person to raise their volume. Focus, on getting your message out, nice and clear, at an even tone, and a soft volume. You will learn to communicate better with people, and, people will communicate, better with you. It is known that you hear a whisper better than a shout. Try whispering to your loved ones. They will pay more attention, they will want to hear what you are whispering about. Their ears will tune in instead of blocking your voice out.

When I first started dating my husband, Den, although he had a lot of amazing great qualities, he had a challenge with communication skills—every other word out of his mouth was a low vibration. I would cringe when I would hear him. I grew up in a household that was very peaceful, and never used curse words. Den has the typical Brooklyn attitude— he comes off as a grizzly bear, but inside, he is a sweet, loving, teddy bear. When we were dating, we would always get into arguments, on how he spoke to me or other people; his tone was harsh. I'd be reprimanding him, like he was my child. Our friends thought we were comical, but it would bother me. Before I knew better, his words got inside me, and I would physically and mentally get ill. I even went to a psychologist, when we were dating. His temperament was affecting me, so much. I loved Den, but I couldn't take his loud demeanor. The psychologist suggested that I end our relationship, and said, I would be miserable if I continued. I broke up with him many times, and he would be so apologetic, and he would make me laugh. I kept hearing the words the angel whispered in my ear when I first met him: "This is the man you're going to marry." I used to question the angel, all the time. I then thought, "If I am marrying this man, I will have to learn how to deal with him." I learned to put myself in a bubble, where the words could not get inside me. It also bothered me when I would hear him talk harshly to others; they weren't protected in a bubble. As harsh as Den could be, is as fun and loving as he could be. His humor and his kind ways won me over. Den does make people laugh wherever we go; they love his humor. He has come a long way in 36 years, and he constantly tells me, how grateful, he is for me, in his life. I know, I was given the challenge to help him, and yet Den has helped me in so many ways unimaginable. As harsh as his words could be at times, his loving, supportive words outweigh the negative ones. There is not a day that he doesn't say, "I Love you." He'll even send those words in a text. He has brought me the love, the care, and the support I was dreaming of. His support allowed me to become the stronger, more assertive person that I am today. God puts people together for a reason. Like Ying and Yang, where there is a lot of similarities, there is a portion that is totally different, but it helps complete the whole circle. No couple is totally perfect; you just have to work through bumps in the road. I feel it is worth it. The grass isn't always greener on the other side; it may have a lot more weeds. The earlier you set the rules, the better the relationship. Don't let children take over your relationship; your partner will feel left out. Pay attention, to how you are speaking, to each other—don't blurt out negative hurtful words, in the heat of an argument. No name calling! A very low vibration only brings negative results. You, are better off not saying anything, if it's not going to be nice. Respect each other, forgive each other, release the negative energy. Never go to bed mad, it does you more damage inside—say, "I love you," to each other. Love is the healer. Keep the love vibration between you.

I am sure you know right from wrong. Words could become abusive. Speaking in a rude, demeaning way is so wrong on all accounts. You were created by the King of all Kings. You are Royalty. Use your Royal tongue to speak words of Love. Don't go around saying: I hate this; I hate that; I hate you; I hate myself;

I hate him; I hate her; I hate everyone; etc. Cancel/ Delete! Every time you say the word *hate*, your vibration goes so low. It's such an ugly, demeaning, hurtful word. *Hate* diminishes your power every time you say it. Remember: Like attracts Like, Hate attracts Hate. It will attract hateful things to you. Erase hate from your vocabulary. A better word to replace that word is dislike. Better yet, don't mention anything or anyone you don't like; you are giving the thing or person energy. *"The best word spoken is the one that is not."*

Pay attention to what you put on the radio or TV in the morning, at home, in the car, or the office. I don't suggest that you listen to the news, especially CNN . . . Continually Negative News. Yes, it's good to be aware of what is going on, but don't base your life around it. Most of the time you can't do anything about it, and it is very sad, so why let it consume your good energy. It will send you into fear or anger mode. Each of your cells will feel it. The cons outweigh the pros when watching or listening to negative news. This is why so many people are suffering with anxiety and depression. You may get so consumed and fill your whole body with fears, doubts, and worry, you will shut down mentally, physically and spiritually. You are so much better off, listening to something soothing; you will still, get the news from others. Don't dwell on it. Negative news puts stress in your body, sending it into fight or flight, and your adrenal glands start to overwork, causing havoc to your body. Keep the news off! If you must watch TV, watch it for learning and laughter. I am hoping one day there will be stations with only positive news. This will put people in a healing, uplifting mode.

Laughter is the best medicine. Notice how you feel when you go to a comedy club, or when you get together with friends, and you're having a lot of fun and laughs—you feel great! Stress just floats out of your body. Start listening to some jokes. When you start laughing and feeling relaxed, you will attract more fun in your life. It's a great cycle: the more you are happy, the more happiness you attract, the more you laugh, the more laughter you will attract. Start by listening to jokes, and slightly tilt your head back and let out a big "Ha, Ha, Ha," and a big "Ho, Ho, Ho." Feel how it feels! You will amuse yourself!

Sound is also very important. What type of music are you listening to? There are tests showing different types of music have a different reaction in your body. Sound vibrates through your whole body, into every single one, of your trillions of cells. Certain music, causes havoc in your body. Take notice how your body reacts towards certain sounds. Do an experiment with the different types of music. Your body will let you know, which types of music, will make you feel, more relaxed and upbeat, or uneasy and stressed. Pay attention to all the sounds around you. Don't subject your body to any sounds you don't like. What is the sound of your alarm in the morning? Is it loud and annoying? If so, change it to something a little more soothing. After your alarm button goes off, hit the snooze button. This is your time, to reflect gratitude, that you got up this morning, and for all the wonderful people, and opportunities in your life. Find something to be grateful for. This starts the magnet to a better day. Try to go to your house of worship weekly. You may feel like you don't need to go anywhere to feel God's presence, and that is true. It is good to listen to the words spoken, as they usually have a message for you. The feeling tone, of the music that is played, is invigorating to each one of your cells. You should feel amazing, when you come out of your house of worship; if not, find another one that will invigorate you.

Gratitude is the start to more blessings. Say, "thank you," with a smile, to every person that does a service for you, and watch their reaction. It will usually, put a little smile, on their face. Say "thank you," out loud, to God and your angels; they will be happy and will start working double time for you. If your grateful list, seems very small, right now, you are in need for some changes. Up until now, it's a reflection, of your gratitude, your words, and your actions. You need to change it up! Today is a new day. From this day forward, you are going be grateful for all the little blessings. The gates of abundance will open up for you. Take notice when you're grateful for all the little things . . . the big things will follow. "Keep Gratitude in your Attitude!"

Every sound and word, has a vibration, that affects every one of the trillion cells, in your body. You are made up of over 75% water, and water, is the most programmable solution, on the earth. Dr. Emoto did an experiment with two jars of water. On one of the jars, he wrote *Love;* on the other jar, he wrote *Hate.* After a week, the difference in the two jars was amazing. The *Love* jar was crystal clear; the *Hate* jar was mucky and dirty. This experiment, is a reflection, of what goes on in your body from words and sounds that get absorbed. Put an imaginary shield or bubble around your whole self—only let in what you want. Always be in protection mode; you have the power.

I hope this chapter helped you to get into the habit of paying attention to your words that you are saying and writing. Pay attention to what others are saying to you. Refute what you don't like, cancel/delete, or turn the channel. Words can be like a sword—put that weapon away. Words backfire. Choose words that are life giving, that keep your heart filled with love. Never say, "My heart is broken," or "My heart is breaking." Instead, protect it, and say, "My heart is consumed with love." In the next chapter, we will speak of the highest frequency, which is number one in your Royal Flush to keep your kingdom going. Protect your *royal kingdom* from any negativity getting in. Surround yourself with the *Love vibration, 528 hrz*; listen to it daily on YouTube. You could listen while you are sleeping; you will receive a subliminal message. Now that you have amped up the power of your words, let's amp up the power of your *Love.* Let's set your Love on fire! Keep your flame burning with Love. You will attract more of it.

POWER PAGE . . . AMP UP YOUR POWER!

(Write Your Thoughts, Words and Affirmations)

_____

_____

_____

_____

_____

_____

_____

_____

_____

_____

_____

_____

_____

_____

_____

_____

_____

_____

_____

CHAPTER 4

THE POWER OF YOUR LOVE AND GRATITUDE

Love is the highest frequency you could vibrate in. LOVE stands for *Living One Vibrational Energy*. Love is the highest state of consciousness; it represents the 5th dimension, the heavens. We are all connected through love. Love is the conqueror of all evil. If you fill yourself with Love, there is no room for evil to move in. The same goes for when you shut yourself down from being loved or giving love— you are allowing negativity to move in. Not purposely, I am sure. I am bringing you awareness of something that is very important. People can't live in a healthy stage without love. Your whole being needs love. Love is extremely important, right up there with oxygen and water. Love is pure. Love is kind. Love is caring. Love is never jealous or envious. Love is very healing.

Everyone is searching for love, but you are looking in the wrong places. Love is inside you; it's been there all along. You are not going to find love in a strip club. Although it may be pleasurable, it's not love. You may think love is feeling an affection for someone else, or that love is something you could fall into or fall out of. Real, true love comes from an understanding of who you are. Loving yourself, is top on the list, for awakening your power. When you learn naturally, to love yourself, you will draw true love to you. It brings you a confidence when you love yourself. Always look your best. Clean yourself up for yourself. How do you expect others to love you, if you don't love yourself? Personal hygiene is very important. A good haircut makes such a difference.

I have been a licensed cosmetologist since I was 18 years old. I love making people feel good, with a great haircut, or some color, to wash away the gray. I remember when I was around 18 years old, I used to go to this older lady's home to do her hair; she was in her nineties. I used to cut and color her hair. I remember, when I was done, she would look into this large hand held mirror, that I carried in my haircutting bag, she had such a smile on her face. I loved seeing her smile. At first, I used to think, "Why does she bother doing her hair?" She really didn't go out much. Then, after a while, I was thinking, "I want to be just like her at that age, looking good and loving myself." Now, with my knowledge of thinking and knowing, I keep the vision that I will be even better, and more vain. I will drive myself weekly to the salon to get my hair done, and pamper myself. I vision coming home to my love, Den, and going out to dinner and a show for date night. When you look good, you feel good, even, if it is just for yourself. Your thoughts and feelings count!

Life is Love and Love is Life. Do you love the life you're living? Love gives you the ability to let go of the past and move forward. Let go of any negative images of yourself, that you have been dragging around, up until now. You are taught to hold onto the past, and use it, as an excuse, for your currant patterns of action. If you come from a dysfunctional family, that is not who you are, unless you accept it. If you live in self-pity and blame others for your living conditions, you are accepting your circumstances. Your power is dormant. You lost connection to the infinite, like you would lose connection to the internet. God helps those who help themselves, and you need to awaken the connection. You have been using your past to dictate your future, up until now. God Loves You! He wants you to be happy. Keep the vision of what you want. Life will challenge you as you develop new thoughts, words, and habits. Your physical self will want to stay in the land of the familiar. Your spirit is always seeking for more. Love is your guiding hand. Love is like someone is holding your hand to take the first step. Just like when I took hold of my grandson's hand to walk; I couldn't make him walk but, after he took his first step, he took another, and another, because he had the support of my hand. When he let go of my hand, he couldn't do it on his own, yet. You never have to fear that you are alone. God will carry you, if he has to; just stay in service for him. Surround yourself with loving people. Stay in an inspiring, loving, influencing sphere of people.

Love is being in service to others to bring them love. When I was young, I had a vision of owning a gym with a hair salon in it. Helping people feel good and look good was always a great feeling; it warmed my heart. It's funny; my vision came very close. I started teaching at different gyms, and I owned a hair salon in 2010 with my daughter Angelica. In 2012, we decided to close up shop; we both had different visions. Your dreams and visions could change along the way. Never think of yourself as a failure for trying—you're a failure if you don't try. Always do your best, and you will be proud of yourself, even when things start changing. When one door closes, don't just stand behind it—open another door. God always has plans for you; you just have to stay in service. Stay in the flow of things. Don't try to paddle up the current, trying to hold onto where you were; the big waves help you rise higher to the next level, and get you safely to shore into the next chapter of your life. The important thing is to stay in love with life, and life will stay in love with you. Trust the process.

When you are not loving yourself, your inner powers diminish and start thinking more negative and lower vibrational thoughts and feelings. If you say, "I don't need love," you are just fooling yourself, and you are pushing love away. If you say, "No one loves me," you are also pushing it away. The best way to receive love, is to give love. Give love unconditionally. Look at yourself in the mirror, take notice of all the good qualities, and be grateful for them. Now look again, and vision the perfect you. Don't dwell from a negative point of view; focus and feel from a positive point of view — start owning the new you. Remember, nothing is impossible, unless you believe that it is. This takes me to a story I read about a prince and a sculpture: The prince hired an artist to make a sculpture of himself. The prince had a hunchback from scoliosis, and he appeared very shallow in his looks. The artist, on the other hand, made the prince a full life-size sculpture of himself, and he made him look handsome, strong, and confident, without any back issues. The prince didn't put it out where everyone could see it because he felt embarrassed that it didn't look like him. He put it in his own private garden, where he looked at it everyday. Then he started imitating the pose. He continued imitating the pose and, within a few years, he really started to look like the sculpture. The power of the mind is unquestionable. Envision the *you* that you want. Have a picture or sculpture that you want to imitate, and look at it every day. Keep that vision beyond any doubt. You are the master sculptor. Know that you are always perfect in God's eyes.

Just simple acts of kindness, for yourself and for others, awakens the Love within you. You have so much love in your heart, but you have the flame, down low. Close your eyes, envision going into your heart and turning up the flame. Envision your heart radiating with a golden radiant glow; start feeling that warmth. Take a deep breath in of; love, joy, peace, happiness and forgiveness. Let it consume every cell;

hold it a second. Then blow out anger, hatred, pain, greed and jealousy—let it all go. Feel the tension leaving your heart; feel the love filling up your heart. Do the breaths a few times. Love is a living energy; send it out to others that you love, that need a little extra love. Keep love flowing, and it will always flow back to you.

Sometimes, love comes when you least expect it, but you do have to expect it coming and own the feeling. I remember, asking God for a nice, fun, loving, respectable family guy, one that was very handy like my dad, loved children, and would show me lots of love. Life is always giving us lessons to learn by. My parents taught my three brothers and I great family values, I am so grateful for the loving bond we have between us. The one thing I was lacking was hearing the words, "I love you," from my parents. I have to say that really bothered me. Especially when I heard other parents saying it to my friends. Although my parents showed love in so many ways, they never said it. I was looking for love. I was looking to hear those words, and I knew, one day, I would find it. God doesn't always answer right away, and sometimes it's when you least expect it; it's all in his time. You just need to put out the vision of what you want, and stay in that vibration.

I went out, one Thursday night, to Club 231, August 6th, 1981, with my girlfriend, Sandy. I had just turned 18 years old, in July. I remember saying to Sandy, as we were walking into the club, "What's the sense if I meet someone tonight? Tomorrow, I am going upstate for two weeks." Well, I guess the angels have humor. I always spent most of my time on the dance floor because I loved dancing, and still do. I had gone to the ladies' room to cool off, as I was walking back to the dance floor, this guy (Den) says, "You look pretty tonight." The way he said it, was like, I knew him. I kept looking at him, over my left shoulder, trying to figure out, where I knew him from. Then, there was a moment; I looked, and I didn't see him anymore. I suddenly, felt a tap on my right shoulder. I turned, and looked, to see who it was, in my surprise, it was him. He said, "Are you looking for someone?" I was so embarrassed, and giggling, at the same time. We went dancing, on the dance floor, for a while, then we went outside to cool off. I remember, standing under a light, and a little bell rang, and a little small voice said, "This is the man you are going to marry." I know it sounds really strange, and I did keep questioning those angels, because I really didn't like his temperament, like I spoke about in the chapter before, about the Power of Words. God and the angels know best, they gave me a man that continually says he loves me on a daily basis. I am with the same man, for 36 years, and I still thank God and his angels every day for doing such a great job. God and the Infinite Universe are always working for your highest, best interest, even when things don't always look like they are. Remember: *say what you want and want what you say*; you are postulating your life daily. Put your order in like you are ordering from a menu. Plant the seeds today of what you want tomorrow.

What were you taught at an early age about love? Did you grow up hearing "I love you?" If you didn't, you might continue life not expecting it. I don't think my parents heard it growing up; that's how things were, but that doesn't mean it was right. Life becomes what you accept and what you expect. If you don't like something, say or do something about it, sooner than later. Don't accept something, if you don't want it. Cancel/delete the thought. In life, you will regret the things you didn't do, more so, than the things you have done. If you want things to change, you have to change. There came a time in my adulthood life, after I had my children, that I finally told my parents how I felt about them not saying "I love you," and how it bothered me, that I couldn't say it to them. I said it, so freely to my husband, my children, my friends, and my relatives, but I couldn't say "I love you" to my parents. It was such a relief, after I was able to tell them, what was bothering me. Now we always say "I Love You" to each other, and it makes me feel really good. If there is any tension in your family, it is really mandatory to resolve the issues. If not, it could cause a "dis/ease" in your body. The tension gets stored up somewhere. Forgiveness is the release of the tension and the dis-ease of the body.

Love really makes the world go around. The whole planet vibrates at a Love frequency of 528 hrz. The sun gives off, a vibrational frequency of 528 hrz. Ever notice, how great you feel with just a few minutes of absorbing the sun rays. The sun is healing with its vibration, it gives you vitamin D, it's good for your bones, and reduces cholesterol. A tree also vibrates at a love frequency of 528 hrz. There is also truth, when they say, "Go hug a tree." When you are feeling a little lack of love, go connect with nature or an animal; it will fill the void. People turn to other fulfillments when they are really looking for love.

Lack of love causes many dis/eases, especially anxiety, depression, and heart issues. Never say someone is breaking your heart. You are sending energy to those words. I used to say it myself, when I heard sad news. I was starting to get a heart murmur. I refrained from saying "that breaks my heart." Cancel/Delete! Think about it; you don't want a broken heart, and neither do I. So let's not say it! It's funny, I no longer have the heart murmur.

Really start paying attention to what you are saying about love. Notice how your love life is and if it is a reflection of what you have been saying or thinking. If you constantly say, "Leave me alone," or "I want to be left alone," is that what you really mean? That creates loneliness. You will push people away. Reframe from saying those words. Say only what you really mean and want. You really want more Love. Tell God what you want, as you're dosing off to sleep, after your gratitude prayers.

Are you feeling you are not good enough for love? God loves you unconditionally! No matter what you have done, you are loved. You have so many people around you that love you, even if they don't say "I love you."

Try sending out warm, caring particles of love to others. Love is energy, so you could send love telepathically through your warm loving thoughts. Love is taking an interest in other people's wellbeing. Change your focus from yourself to others. When you help others, you are actually helping yourself. Same goes: if you hurt others, you are hurting yourself. Choose love.

We are all meant to have a loving partner, except those sworn to celibacy; they are content with God's love. Intimacy is so important. Always keep your love connection fun. Compliment each other daily. At least one hug and kiss a day minimal is my recommendation, if possible. A hug actually releases stress. A hug a day keeps the doctor away, because we all need a release. Grab a hold of your partner's hand when they don't expect it. It brings up the vibration of both your souls. It is not just about the act of sex. It is that vibrational connection between two people that becomes explosive. Take notice of the vibration between the two of you.

How's your sex life? You are never too old; it's just your thoughts. It's even proven. Many people in nursing homes are still having sex, they are senile, and they don't know, they're old. Their negative thoughts, or paradigms, are not getting in their way. Too many people put too much stress on the performance. Start with the vibration. The act of touching sends an energy through the both of you. Learn to connect to that energy, first. Everything else will transpire on its own.

To secure a better life of intimacy, make sure you are both keeping your royal kingdoms healthy. Loving yourself is ace. If you don't love yourself, how can you expect to love your partner? Work on it. Do your deep breathing exercises daily. Stay properly hydrated with ionized alkaline water at all times, that in itself gives you a higher vibration. Ladies, it will help regulate your hormones and keep your libido happy. Men, drink a big glass of ionized water and take the nutritional supplement L-Arginine, 1000mgs, one hour before intimacy, and it will keep your confidence up! Being intimate is the utmost being and has a very high frequency, because it is the joining of two energies as one. It is very powerful when you make the connection and become one with your partner. Keep the love young and alive. Love never ages. I highly recommend having date night at least once a week. Keep that dating feeling of when you first met. I try my best to keep that going. Don't let life get in the way, make it priority. There is no reason not to keep the flame going. Age is just a number and an excuse—cancel/delete any negative thoughts! You are as old as you want to be. Many married couples don't think it's important as they get older to have intimacy. Health wise, it is very important. When you don't have the intimacy, you start drifting apart and sometimes look for other things for the void. It is your mindset, on how you look at things. Don't be so critical of yourself or your partner. Focus on your good qualities. Focus on their good qualities. Try building their confidence up instead of tearing it down. Remember, words hurt, and you don't want to hurt the one you love. Keep up the attraction; always try to look your sexy best. Look in the mirror, and make some adjustments, if you're not liking what you see. Say daily, "I am tight, firm, and sexy." Believe and watch yourself transform. You have the power to change anything. Keep your focus on what you want; cancel/delete any thoughts, you don't want. Start working out. It helps bring up your self-esteem, and the happy hormones. When you start paying attention to your partner, they will start paying attention to you. Be kiddish! Spirit loves fun! Give them a little pinch on the butt, give them a hug from behind, when they least expect it, grab their hand at the movie theater. It's the little things that mean a lot. Men, open the car door for your woman. I love that; my husband still does it when we go out on date night. Give love, and you will receive so much love back. Love will always be in the air, and it is intoxicating; it is a natural high. "You don't have to be young and vibrant to make love—making love makes you young and vibrant."

When you fill your whole self with love, you stand protected. God is Love. You fill yourself with the confidence of knowing.

In the pure frequency of love, there is gratitude. Gratitude is a state of being grateful and satisfied. The way to connect to God's love is to start showing gratitude. Gratitude is the amplifier to love. Learn to always have gratitude in your attitude. When you are grateful for the little things, God will continue giving you more and more. Everyone likes to be thanked, even God. What continues to keep your power of love generating high, is continually, being in a state of gratitude. Gratitude is a high frequency; it keeps life flowing and accelerating for more and more abundance.

Thanksgiving is the giving of thanks. The love and the joy of family is very gratifying. Every Thanksgiving for the last 25 years, we have always gone upstate. I am so grateful to my parents for keeping that tradition. Always try to keep the love of the family flowing and traditions going. Family is a strong bond that you should never let anything or anyone come between. Family is love. Always try to work out, any differences, it is not healthy to keep anything, unsettled. It brings a dis/ease to every family member. Always strive for everyone to be at ease. Everything and anything could be worked out with the love of God.

You may ask: If God is love, why are so many people living with hatred, poverty, dis/ease, and living on the streets? It is because they are living in a state of lack—lack of love, lack of faith, lack of trusting, lack of confidence, and the lack of knowing the power within them is greater than any circumstance that is around them. You cannot work on the world's challenges until you work on your own kingdom within yourself. It is your soul's purpose to be in service of love and light. Darkness does not have a chance when you turn on the light. Namaste means: "May the light in me Honor the Light in You." Love is the amplifier of more love and light. The more you love yourself, the more love you will see, radiating from your beautiful earth. Turn up the flame of love in your heart.

In the next chapter, I am going to speak about your *Royal Flush* that keeps your *Royal Kingdom* glorified with God. Love is the Ace of Hearts in your royal flush. Love is number one—when used right, it is above royalty. Love keeps your heart at a certain rhythm, the vibration of 528 hrz. A life without love is very bitter and gloomy. You don't need anyone to start the process for love; it's very simple. Love is not outside you; love is inside you. Magnetize it. Look in the mirror and say three little words daily: "I Love You." If you know anyone living with bitterness, say: "I Love You." Watch them brighten up. Turn on the light for others in the dark—Love is the light; Love is the laughter; Love is the beauty; Love is the healing; Love is Ace! Now that the power of your Love is amped up, lets go onto the next chapter to learn how to amp up the Power of *Oxygen*.

POWER PAGE . . . AMP UP YOUR POWER!

(Write Your Thoughts, Words and Affirmations)

_____

_____

_____

_____

_____

_____

_____

_____

_____

_____

_____

_____

_____

_____

_____

_____

_____

_____

_____

_____

_____

_____

_____

CHAPTER 5

THE POWER OF OXYGEN, BREATHING AND EXERCISING

Oxygen, is a key essential. An essential, is something that the body doesn't make but needs it to survive. Oxygen is a living energy that is breathing you. It is Prana, a life force. Without the energy of oxygen, you no longer have life. Oxygen is King!

I am going to use a fun analogy to help simplify the importance of the essentials of what the body needs. I want you to think of a *Royal Flush*, and we are using the *red hearts* to symbolize your heart. Ace of hearts, as mentioned in the chapter before, is Love. Oxygen is the King of Hearts, Water is the Queen of Hearts, Enzymes is the Jack of Hearts, and Exercise is the 10 of Hearts. I want you to keep this analogy, these are royalties, to keep your kingdom flowing. When your kingdom is not doing well, hold your royal subjects responsible. Look first at the Ace: is there Love and God in your heart? Look next at the King: are you taking deep breaths into your belly, and deep exhales, exhaling the toxins out? Then look at the Queen: did you drink a minimal 80 ounces of clean water? Then look at the Jack: did you eat your minimal 4 fruits and 5 vegetables? Now check with the 10 of hearts: although it's not a royal subject, moving is important—10,000 steps daily required for everyone. Check all these before you run to the doctor, if you're not feeling well. Your body (kingdom) will let you know when you are depleted in any of these five royal subjects. They are key essentials for keeping your body fueled for manufacturing the best power output. It is your obligation to fuel your body with what it needs. You cannot live without any of them, especially the King, Oxygen.

Breathing is key. I feel that if you are suffering with obesity, you are most likely oxygen deficient. You may be shallow breathing, only breathing into your chest like many do. Your entire metabolism will be affected. Oxygen awakens the power to a younger, healthier, firmer, tighter, sexier you.

Breathing is the Prana of Life. Oxygen helps your cells metabolize nutrients and fat for energy. Oxygen brings up your metabolism, and helps repair your cells, organs, and bones. Breathing is also a key for the elimination of waste, toxins, and fat— something that you might not connect breathing with. When your body can't eliminate the toxins properly, they will get stored up into your fat cells. Your fat cells are actually protecting your body from getting overly toxic from the toxins. *"Carbon dioxide is the most abundant of all the end products of metabolism"* . . . Dr. A. Guyton. An important observation that you should make is that carbon dioxide is a byproduct waste that the body needs to eliminate. Think about this, and ask yourself, "Why would I put carbon dioxide back into my body with carbonated drinks?" You know your body is going to go into protection mode, it creates a fat cell around the carbon; it thinks of it as a toxin—it can't be utilized. That's why when you burp, you think it's a good thing, but it really isn't. Now this is going to really "wow" you. The best kept secret is to utilize breath to release stagnate energy and impurities from your cells. When you engage the navel center and the solar plexus, you super oxygenate the blood and help balance the nervous system, all while getting tighter, firmer, sexier abs. I have learned this as a yoga teacher—Kundalini Yoga, "Breath of Fire;" Greer Childers with "Body Flex;" Jill R. Johnson with "Oxycising."—you could disintegrate fat from deep breathing exercises. *"Fat leaves the body through carbon dioxide. You can increase your capacity for oxygen/carbon dioxide exchange by breathing more deeply. You can* burn *extra fat with increased breathing"* . . . Jill R. Johnson. *"This means, by increasing oxygen, you can bring your own body's metabolic process into balance"* . . . R. Dunham. Science and research has shown that melting pounds off is all in the exhale. This is vital information.

I personally used to concentrate a lot more on my breathing exercises by doing the breath of fire all the time, popping in a video and doing Body Flex, and doing "Oxycise" with my daughter Angelica. We got great results: nice, firm, tight abs. I really didn't know the science behind it back than; I just knew that it worked. Now that it is many years later, I have stopped practicing the breathing and have packed on 20 lbs. that should be released by the time the book is published. A little voice inside me said, "Go back to doing the breathing exercises, and incorporate it with core strengthening Pilates moves." I came up with X-Halates, a combo of exhaling and Pilates. I have the knowledge of why it will work, and God wants me to incorporate it into my book. When you're exhaling, your body is concentrating on getting the carbon dioxide waste out. I want you to have the vision, as you are exhaling, you are blowing out thousands of fat cells. They are disintegrating in the air, and you are getting tighter and firmer and sexier abs, and a whole tighter version of yourself. This is why aerobics work so well—you're exhaling a lot. When you concentrate on the exhale, you automatically inhale deeper. You could do this technique while lying in bed in the morning, or in the shower, sitting at your desk, stopped at a light in your car, sunning, or virtually anywhere and anytime you want to. There is no specific age requirements. You could start at any age. The great thing is, once you learn this technique, you could continue to do it throughout the rest of your life. It helps regulate your bowels, it will help you breath better, it will help you sleep better, and you will have better mental clarity. Oxygen is abundant and free; the best things in life are free. It doesn't need a script or anyone's approval, and oxygen doesn't counteract with anything.

I remember, one evening, when I was around nine years old. I was reading a Nancy Drew mystery story; I loved reading her books. I also remember I was gasping for my next breath, something that we all take for granted. I had severe asthma and I didn't have an inhaler. I never used an inhaler. I remember looking into the light of my night stand next to my bed and praying to God to help me breathe, I made a deal with him. I told him, "God, help me breathe, and I will help You." That night, I don't remember what happened. I did have a good night's sleep, and I did wake up the next morning refreshed. My asthma continued to get better and better; after the age of 16, it was gone. Awakening my power of knowing something greater than myself, and learning the power of oxygen, water, enzymes, and exercise, contributed to my miraculous healing.

Many people breathe wrong, and you may be one of them. Watch a baby as he or she breathes. Take notice as the baby inhales, the baby's stomach expands. As the baby exhales, the stomach contracts. Now put your hand on your stomach and inhale. Do you feel your chest expanding or your stomach? The correct way to breathe is, inhale through your nose, into the stomach and rib cage, and when you exhale, you're deflating the stomach, contracting the abs, belly button to spine. Breathing correctly is very important. Breathing helps every trillion of your cells in your body. When you are in a more stressed, fearful, or panic mode, the breaths become very shallow. Scientifically, the way you breathe affects your heart, lungs, brain, arteries, and blood flow. Stress signals the triglyceride levels to go up in the blood, causing more red blood cells, which clogs up the capillaries; the blood becomes coagulated, restricting proper blood flow, which then interferes with proper oxygen delivery to the cells and causes your heart to have to pump extra hard. Then you panic more because you can't breathe. It is a vicious cycle and, when this is happening, I recommend getting ionized alkaline water in there as soon as possible because it helps bring in the oxygen to the blood to start unclogging it. It becomes like "Roto-Rooter" and gets rid of the clogs. It gets the blood flowing because the ionized water is micro-clustered. It will help you within 10 minutes, as I have seen by an experiment done by an immunologist.

This brings me to a story with a friend of mine, Gino, who at the time was on dialysis. Den and I, and Gino and Alyson went to dinner. After dinner, we went back to their home and had dessert. Gino had picked up some freshly made, assorted donuts earlier that day. He had a cannoli donut and, shortly after eating it, he had to say goodnight to us and go upstairs to get hooked up to dialysis. Within an hour, while we were watching a movie, he calls us from his cell saying how bad he feels. Since he had such a heavy meal, the same thing started to happen to him. From eating a heavy meal, the body does the same thing—his digestion went into stress mode. Blood starts to coagulate from stress. Everything starts to slow down. He started panicking and called 911 emergency. I kept telling him to drink the ionized water, but he wouldn't. I really insisted and told him he had nothing to lose; the emergency vehicle was on its way, so they would help him. So, just to shut me up, he drank the 11.5, which is the highest alkalinity. By the time, they were at the door, he was feeling better. We all insisted he go to the hospital to get checked. He was cleared and discharged a couple hours later. Soon after that, my girlfriend, Alyson, donated her kidney to Gino; they are both doing great. Gino went from taking over 40 pills a day to being down to about 6. They are both advocators of the ionized alkaline water. When you are not getting enough oxygen, you will feel at *dis/ease*, a state of being when you are not at ease. You will feel fatigued, tired, and lifeless. When you are in an emergency state, always call 911. Then check your royal subjects first: check King of Oxygen and Queen of Water intake, or Jack of Enzymes—it could possibly save your life before the ambulance gets to you. Do not take this information lightly; it is very important. You will amp up your power when your body is flowing correctly. Oxygen, Water, and Enzymes . . . You O.W.E. it to yourself.

If you are not getting enough oxygen, your metabolism will slow down, and you will start packing on the pounds. You will look for magic pills, potions, lotions, diet plans, or starvation, but nothing seems to work long term. You are born to move. The more you move, the more you will feel better. Movement keeps everything flowing. Movement helps awaken the sleeping power within. When you are moving at an increased rate, you manufacture more serotonin, which is the happy hormone. When you get the serotonin going, it feels like a natural high. It really helps combat anxiety and depression.

Exercise and movement are great for everyone of all ages. Exercise calls your body for more oxygen, so you breathe more. You are never too old to start exercising, and your body will thank you for it. The "10 of hearts" is exercise. Recommended by the heart association is 10,000 steps daily. I track my own steps on a fitbit; it's like a watch. Exercise is important to do, and you will feel like a 10 when you do something daily. I highly recommend you do an hour of moving around daily. It doesn't have to be all at once. If you can't move around, at least do some deep breathing exercises.

Too many people these days are sitting way too much, for long periods of time. Everything becomes stagnant and gets sluggish. I know, for myself, the more I am up and about doing things, the more energy I seem to have. I also notice when I am sitting too much, like when I go to 3 day seminars, I get more tired. The key is to stay balanced. Don't over exert yourself, but do a little more, and you will get your adrenaline up. Just walking does not count for total body movement. Remember, use it or lose it; bending and twisting are very important. When you get up in the morning, do a couple of stretches. It is best to get in a routine that is best for you.

Pilates is a great form of exercising that awakens your core. Joseph Pilates came up with the technique of Pilates in the 1920s, and he taught his troops the techniques. Pilates was used to keep his military troops healthy. They were the only ones that didn't get wiped out by influenza. Joseph Pilates' troops were strong and healthy. When keeping your core strong, you keep your abs from getting sluggish, which in turn helps your back. Keep visualizing nice, firm, tight abs. Thinking and feeling is believing.

I created a form of Pilates; it's called X-Halates. I devised it, utilizing different core exercises and putting concentration on the deep inhales and deep exhales. I have been teaching this method for over 13 years in different gyms that I have worked at. The uniqueness is in the deep inhales on extensions, and deep exhales as you twist, bend, or contract. This method of combining both really helps strengthen, tone, and firm up the abs and core. I plan on making a DVD one of these days, on the specific movements that are beneficial for the whole body, they truly helped me. These moves have kept me feeling very flexible, pain free, and youthful. Let me show you an easy exercise that will really make a difference if you practice it daily or at least a couple of times weekly. It is very simple and easy. I came up with it to strengthen my abs while I had severe back pain. I knew that keeping my core strong relieved pressure from my lower back. I want to pass this great knowledge onto you. Lie on your stomach, face down, hands under your forehead, and get into a relaxed position. I want you to take a deep inhale through your nose, and bring that oxygen down to your belly, expanding your belly like an accordion or a balloon, and hold; then, blow out the air through your mouth, and visualize the accordion closed or the balloon deflated, as you are doing this, pull your belly button off the floor, towards your spine; your hips and rib cage stay down. Envision your belly button is being pulled up with a string towards the ceiling, and hold it like that, making a bridge while a little match box car drives under it. Hold about 8 seconds, release by inhaling, and again expand the abs and rib cage, and repeat it a few times. It's a little thing that really makes a difference. If you can't lie on your stomach, lie on your back and do the same: inhale and expand; when you exhale, deflate your abs and pretend someone is pulling your belly button towards the floor (your spine), while your hips shift slightly up. Hold that position about 8 seconds and inhale through your nose to release. Drink plenty of water a half hour before and right after to keep every joint and vertebra lubricated. If you have pain, and you feel you have rusty joints, you are dehydrated. Water is your lubrication, like oil is to machinery. Your whole vertebrae is like a stack of jelly donuts, one on top of the other; when there is not enough water, the donuts flatten out, it causes friction and pain. Inflate them with water. Keep the love, oxygen, water, enzymes, and exercising flowing, and you will have a healthy spine.

Dancing is a really great way to turn up the power. I love dancing. When the music is good, it really helps bring up your frequency. Dancing is a great way to let loose and get rid of any particles latching onto your body. Zumba is another form of dancing that has really become popular at the gyms. They are both very beneficial because they combine sound and movement, the two are powerful. Dancing has been around for centuries. You have to shake your arms in the air, and move it, like you just don't care! Dancing gets everything flowing and clears your mind. It is said that after dancing, you have 76% increased mental activity. I feel it's because dancing clears the junk. So, it is good to do before you need to do something with deep concentration.

Spin bike, Kickboxing, and Step classes are also fun to let out some frustration and bottled up tension. I personally never got into jogging but, if you like it, that is great. I find the Elliptical to be easier on the joints and similar to jogging. The trampoline is a great way to get lymph glands circulating. One of my favorites that I use daily is a Vibra Therapy machine. It's great for the lymphatic system and has very low impact. I do my reading on the Vibra Therapy machine; I stand on it for 10 minutes; I sit on it for 10 minutes; I lie on my stomach for 10 minutes; and then I put my palms down on it for 10 minutes. I find it to be less invasive than a trampoline and is also a great way to get the lymph glands circulating. You just stand or sit on it, and a vibration goes through your whole body. It's great for people with limited mobility. It's also great for weight loss, because it helps circulate the toxins out. Drink a big glass of ionized water after doing the exercises to escalate everything out, more efficiently.

You have to find what you enjoy doing. The important thing is to do something. Find a few things that you like and stick to it. It's nice to join a gym because you than have a lot of variety, and it becomes a great place to socialize with others. Communication with others is also very important; it brings up your vibration. At the gym, it's a sharing of energy in the room which uplifts your energy. Try to surround yourself with positive energy. People that smile a lot and send off a good vibration are the ones you want to be around. They will uplift you and hopefully rub off so you start smiling.

Flexibility is also key; the more flexible your spine is, the more youthful you will stay, you will eliminate back issues. You have to move it or lose it. If you don't use certain parts, they start to stiffen up. A great way to start the morning is to stand up and bring your hands up together into a mountain pose, take a big inhale (filling abs like a balloon); then, open those arms and exhale (blowing out, contracting your abs) as you are swan diving to the floor with your arms open wide, and then sweep the floor, crisscrossing your arms as you sweep back up into mountain pose, and repeat around 4 times. Then, on the last one, stay down, and sink deep, deeper, and deepest (blowing out all the air). Let all the tension out, now inhale slowly as you are either rolling up vertebrae by vertebrae, or walk up your legs with your hands, when you get to the top, roll your shoulders up and back. Ahhhh!! That should feel great, if you want an extra bonus, cross one leg over the other, squeeze your gluts tight and your hips forward; lock your thumbs overhead. Inhale up, and exhale bend as you hinge at the hips, bringing your hands down to the floor. Do that about 4 times and then unclasp your thumbs while bent over. Relax your shoulders, neck, and face, then begin inhaling as you are rolling up, or walking up your legs with your hands, when at the top, roll your shoulders up and back, and then switch legs (whichever was in front before is now crossed in the back), and keep your gluts tight and hips forward, and repeat. These are my favorites for opening the hips and keeping the spine youthful; it's very important as you age.

Yoga is a powerhouse. I have been practicing it for over 15 years. It is truly my medicine. It keeps me balanced and connected to my spirit. It makes me feel whole. Yoga turns up your connection to your power within. There are specific moves in yoga, each are very beneficial and have a purpose. Yoga is great for your mind, body, and soul connection. I have seen miraculous connections in a few sessions, the dis/ease of depression and anxiety, a thing of the past. Yoga works on balance, coordination, breathing, flexibility, and core strength. I find it to be a superior treat for your whole being. It helps bring your body to balance and peace. Peace is a mindset. You will learn to master it with Yoga and Meditation.

Meditation is a key to your life. It will open new doors for you. Prayer is you talking to God; meditation is God talking to you. Meditation allows you to hear that small voice that tries to talk to you. You might not hear it because of so many distractions. The reason many people are at dis/ease, is because, you never make time to quiet down and listen. Shut the distractions off around you for at least 10-20 minutes a day. You need peace. It is mandatory for wellbeing. My vision is to create ministries all over, that you could go to, to have that peace, so God may speak to you. It is important to listen. Everyone has a soul purpose. The more at peace you become, the more awakened you become. Your power amps up. A great way to start is through guided meditations, I have a wonderful spiritual instructor at my center that takes you on a journey for an hour, and it is very transformational. Peace is something to strive for. You deserve it.

For older adults, chair yoga is amazing. I also teach it, I love observing my group; I see such a vast improvement in such little time. I see it brings them confidence. Each week they get better and better. Your body is not meant to get old and stiff. Your 30 trillion cells are always reproducing, creating new cells as long as you keep the "Royal Flush" going. Pain is a sure sign of severe dehydration. Thoughts hold onto pain, and chair yoga is a great way to help release the thoughts and flow into movement. The truth is, as you get older, you should do more, not less. Your spirit never ages; your thoughts do. You have to stay in motion. Let your "Royal Flush" keep up your "Royal Kingdom." You could be old at 30 or young at 90—your choice.

Swimming is also great for the young and old. It is great to build up lung capacity. It helped me with my asthma. It is also great for arm and leg coordination. Water is great to exercise in because you don't feel the tension. My dad is in his 80s and he belongs to a center where he goes swimming a couple times a week, in the summer, he swims daily in the lake. My dad's shoulder is getting better and so is his spirit. When you have a limitation, gently work through it; your body wants to heal. Focus on your *Royal Flush,* and age will only be a number. Do a variety of different movements with your arms and legs. Water is such a great stress releaser naturally, so while swimming, just release. To release even more while you're in the water, try to float with your head up or down. Just let your whole self-float, and close your eyes and visualize all your tension releasing into the water. Always make sure you have someone around for safety precautions while you are in the water.

Going walking or hiking outdoors is a great stress releaser. Do some deep breathing. Don't always be concerned about plugging into music; utilize the time to get plugged into your infinite power. While walking do some thinking and visioning. Ask yourself, "What would I love?" Always try to keep yourself in a positive vibration and you will start generating positive ideas, which will bring positive actions, causing positive results.

Just go outside, and go for a walk. Try walking different times of the day. You might notice the fresh morning dew if you go out early. You might notice birds chirping. Just take notice of your surroundings, appreciate your surroundings, and you will awaken something inside. There is a frequency in nature (528hrz) that automatically lifts your spirits. Make sure you always bring water with you to stay properly hydrated.

I love the outdoors. I feel so grateful and blessed that my parents bought a summer home in the country when I was 4 years old. We were a family of 6, and dad was working two jobs. At the time, he couldn't afford to take us on vacations. He was given an opportunity to help out a friend in a bind, and we were able to get an old house on a Lake. Going upstate always felt like such a release from suburban life; we were missing a lot of amenities up there. Years ago, we had no phones or television. We made the best with what we had: we played outside all day on the swings; we went for walks; we fished, and many times we just threw them back; we swam in the lake; at night we played cards, board games, and read books. It was really nice to just go outside and look at all the stars up in the dark sky. I am bringing this up because you could go anywhere, and you could find things to keep you busy, while staying in peace. Turn off the internet and get connected to your infinite.

I have two favorite water sports that I like to do when I go to the lake. One is paddle boating. I paddle boat around the whole perimeter of the lake. It takes me about 3 hours, and I am usually reading a book pertaining to wellness. I have been doing this over 20 years, even when I had my severe, lower back pain. I used to grit through the pain; the worst part was getting up out of the boat after sitting all those hours, but nothing held me back. To me, it was worth it. I was convinced I was going to heal, and movement was going to help me. That was my mindset, and that is what I set out to do. Set your mind to what you want. Cancel/delete anything you don't want. While paddle boating, I love when I come across the lake eagle; flying above me or in a tree; he is the symbol of freedom and independence. This summer a peace came over me when I saw the eagle. I associated the eagle with Mr. Donald J Trump. He wasn't President at the time, but this feeling came over me that he would be and our great nation would regain our freedom and independence. Have trust and faith. Release any negative thoughts.

My other favorite water sport is kayaking. I love kayaking after dinner as the sun is going down and the lake is starting to calm down. It is an amazing feeling being on the lake when all the ripples start to turn into a sheet of glass. Everything becomes still and tranquil. Many times I see a whole school of ducks swimming alongside me—every night is a new adventure. Some nights I stay out there later, I hear the crickets, and I watch the stars start to shine as the sky gets darker and darker. The peace really starts to set in, it becomes a reflection of how my body starts to feel. You too need to find a release. You could even take a lounge chair, put it outside during the warmer nights, and just go out there by yourself and reflect on the wonders of the beautiful Universe. Relax to awaken.

Now that we amped up your oxygen, your breathing, and your exercising, you are ready to amp up your *water intake*, so you can really get things flowing!

POWER PAGE . . . AMP UP YOUR POWER!

(Write Your Thoughts, Words and Affirmations)

_____

_____

_____

_____

_____

_____

_____

_____

_____

_____

_____

_____

_____

_____

_____

_____

_____

_____

_____

_____

CHAPTER 6

THE POWER OF DRINKING WATER

Water is right up there with Oxygen and definitely does not get enough credit; it is a key Essential Nutrient. The body doesn't make water, so you need to drink a lot of water to keep your machinery running. It is essential to get half your body weight in ounces, and for children up to 12 years old, one ounce per pound. Anyone suffering with any health issues also needs one ounce per pound. There are no replacements for water. Every one of your 30 trillion cells needs water. There is some water found in fruits and vegetables because they too are made of 75% water, but you would need to eat a lot of them. Every cell runs on water (not coffee). Water is the conductor of energy, and it carries nutrients throughout the body. Water is the Essence of all Life. Like Mother Earth, she is 75% water, and so are you. In the analogy of your *Royal Flush*, water is the Queen of Hearts. Water is a royal flush in itself and is needed to keep a healthy, happy heart and the rivers and the streams of the body flowing.

As quoted from the book, *Water Cures: Drugs Kill,* by Dr Batmanghelidj, *"There is a medical breakthrough that is not reaching the public through our medical schools or health-maintenance organizations: the discovery that chronic, unintentional dehydration is the primary cause of pain and disease in the human body, including cancer. The reason these traditionally trusted institutions do not celebrate this scientific discovery and refuse to use it to help the sick and the uninsured poor in our society is obvious. There would be no money in it for them."* Dr. Batmanghelidj also believes your body needs 1/2 tsp. of sea salt a day, which he claims to be a missing nutrient, causing many *dis/eases.* Our blood and brain are made of the same consistency of the ocean. When there is a shortage, it causes many unbalances and prevents your organs from working properly. All liquids are not equally used in the body. There could be an abundance of liquid but a shortage of water inside the cells. Many beverages on the market today cause dehydration and acidosis. Water is necessary for every function and organ in your body. Dehydration means low energy reserves in the body. As the body becomes more and more dehydrated, it is forced to break up its bone structure to tap into its stored energy. This is how people develop osteoporosis. Hydrating the body properly does the reverse. Water is the main source of energy to the human body. Dr. Batmanghelidj did not believe in using medications with harmful side effects. It is very disturbing that Dr. Batmanghelidj is no longer here today to advance his studies.

Through all my studies, I find it very shameful that doctors restrict water, and give water pills, while not really having been given the knowledge and all the benefits of water because there is no money to be made in prescribing water. It just does not make sense to me. Many people are severely dehydrated. First thing they do in the hospital is put you on IV, and you start feeling better, and that is because it is water and saline solution. Our bodies were designed perfectly by God to take care of itself. The body will pool up water into an area that is severely inflamed because it is not getting enough water. Water is the body's defense mechanism and is sent out to help heal the area in need. So, logically, it wouldn't make sense to restrict water and prescribe water pills to make the body more dehydrated. I don't understand the logic. It really baffles me. As a Holistic Minister Practitioner, I recommend drinking more water, not less, to help everything flow easier and to eliminate the body's defense to pool up where the body feels it needs more water, and flush out the acid waste. My recommendation is to stay away from all carbonated and sugary drinks that are putting the body into a severe acidosis stage. I find it very odd that those drinks are not restricted but water is. Drink only clean fresh water, and take notice of how your body will start flowing, and the power within you will start generating. Don't get off any meds on your own. Speak to your doctor about your new found knowledge that is not taught to them. I am not discrediting the loving, caring, serving doctors in the medical field; I am just trying to bring awareness to a key essential nutrient that is not mentioned as a key component in the life balance of your bodies, especially that we are 75% water, our brain 80%, and our blood 90%.

Dehydration is the root of many dis/eases. The basis of dis/ease is that the body's organs are in a stagnant, overly acidic environment, and there is too much protein in your tissue. Think of a dirty fish tank. This is a simple analogy of what happens to the body when you don't drink enough water. You're intoxicating your organs in acid waste. Now, would you give the fish (your organs) a pill to fix the problem, or would you simply keep drinking clean fresh water to flush all the waste out? Water keeps everything flowing and helps detox the organs, making them feel revived and fresh. Just like you would have happy fish if the tank was clean, the same analogy holds true when it comes to your organs.

According to the Mayo clinic, the average adult loses more than 10 cups of water a day, simply by breathing, perspiring, and eliminating waste. When you are not able to replenish the water, it could lead to fatigue, which will slow you down and make you feel irritable. Not being properly hydrated will cause constipation; it will pull water from the stool to hydrate your organs that are in need of water, making your stool very difficult to flow out. Being dehydrated will cause digestive issues because you will not be able to secrete enough digestive juices. Simple solution—drink more water!

Aging is the result of cellular water loss. A wrinkle, and hair loss, is a sign of dehydration. 50-75% of Americans are chronically dehydrated. Newborns and infants start out with about 90% water. By the time they are a teen, it could be 70%, and an elder, 50% or less. This has damaging results. The power within you diminishes more and more with less and less water flowing. Water is so important to the brain because it is made of 80% water. Our society has a lot more brain issues than ever before. Studies have shown just 1% water loss causes 5% cognitive disorder; 5% less water loss causes 25% cognitive disorder. So, how important is water to mental illness? I would be safe saying *extremely important*. Do you think a pill would fix that? We need to do something about this now. Everyone has campaigns for different auto-immune issues. The key focus should be on water deficiency. We need to bring water awareness to everyone, starting in our schools. It's the simpler things in life that make the most difference. Children need to stay away from carbonated, sugary drinks and drink more clean, fresh water.

Water is a key nutrient and, without enough water, the best vitamins and minerals cannot be absorbed into the cells. Water is involved in the transfer of data from DNA. Water transports, stabilizes, signals, and hydrates. Drinking water eliminates afternoon fatigue for many individuals. Water helps endurance for athletes, and helps the same person sitting behind a computer all day.

When there is insufficient water, every bodily function and organ suffers and goes into *crisis mode,* and results in *dis/ease* of the body. Symptoms include acne, dry skin, heartburn, constipation, and headaches. When you start drinking the right amount of water, you start to feel better, look better, and have more energy. Every disease can be traced to dehydration.

Water is the most programmable product in the world. Dr. Emoto provides us with data from numerous studies. A powerful thing to do to your water is to bless it with love and lots of energy. Have great thoughts while drinking your water. This is why your thoughts and the environment around you affects your body. Since you are 75% water, and water is programmable, you really need to protect your environment around you and inside you. If you want love and peace, surround yourself with love and peace.

Water is #1 for relieving pain. Pain is a sign the body is dehydrated and inflamed. Picture a red ball of fire, depending on how intense your pain is. When I had my lower back issues at the age of 37, the base of my spine felt like a ball on fire. Would you just throw a pill on the fire and expect results? Add a lot of water to your regimen and watch, and feel the results. Water is the master regulator; it is in charge of all the functions of your body. We do have to be thankful for the pharmaceutical industry because they have intelligently made a pill for every symptom of dehydration and is perfect for people that want a quick fix. Most people like the quick fix. I, on the other hand, gritted through my pain. Through my thoughts, words and actions, I got the results I wanted. Pain free! Many people don't drink water, and with all this knowledge, still won't drink water.

"You can lead a horse to water but you can't make him drink it." This is why the Sick-Care industry is very much needed, and we need to stay in gratitude for them. They are not a disease preventing health care system. Their concern is not to get to the root; their purpose is to relieve the symptoms. They do a great job at that and will never go out of business. My message from God is, "the power within you is greater than any symptom." If you put more power on the pill, your power diminishes. Utilize both to create the outcome you want. Medication is not meant to heal; the Power within is meant to heal. Don't accept anything less. Pain does not exist in your spirit; it is manmade.

Water is the best antihistamine. When you take antihistamines or decongestants, you are dehydrating the body. Dehydration limits proper blood circulation and the removal of waste and allergens from the body. Histamine is a neurotransmitter in charge of water regulation and drought management in your body. *"The Pharmaceutical industry does not possess a single drug that can compete with water as a natural antihistamine. All drugs have side effects; water has none."* . . . Dr. Batmanghelidj. He successfully treated over 3000 patients and came to the conclusion that they all suffered with chronic unintentional dehydration.

When he increased their intake of water, along with 1/2 teaspoon of sea salt, their symptoms went away. When you have the sniffles, or watery eyes, that is a sure sign your body is asking for a glass of water. Give your body what it is crying for — Water!

Water is an essential nutrient that regulates your metabolism and all your physiological functions of your body. If you are overweight, you are most likely dehydrated. Not getting enough water slows down your metabolism. If you are very moody, it is a sure sign of dehydration. Water helps produce and regulate your hormones. This is key; as you are getting older, you want all your hormones and neurotransmitters to be balanced because everything is affected when they are not. You feel totally out of whack! The solution is: drink more water! What you and everyone else does is run for the pills, the creams, or the injections, and not really ever getting to the root cause — WATER! When not receiving enough water, the body reacts in an unbalanced way, causing havoc and dis/ease. Many water deficit dis/eases are just labels given by the pharmaceutical companies. Our society is suffering from not drinking enough good clean water. We need awareness!

You have been brainwashed into accepting that pain and suffering is ok, and is of the norm in your society. Refute this thought! There should be no pain and suffering. There is a natural process in the workings of your body. Your body is created by Intelligence and is designed to heal itself. Drink more Water!

Does this sound too simple? Life was not designed to be complicated. God gave us everything we need to heal. Your thinking Power is key, and you lose the Power as the fluids diminish. It is very important to stay hydrated, next to breathing. In schools, children should have a water break every hour to hydrate their thinking power, and they need to know the importance of water and the relationship it has to their thinking power. When a child is short-tempered and having a little fit, it is usually because they are severely dehydrated. If we educated our children on the importance, we would have less of all the mental dis/eases the children are getting labeled with.

Many people helplessly abandon their power within themselves and turn over their power to the sickness industry. The sickness industry has amazing professionals; unfortunately, they don't have all the answers. If they did, we wouldn't have as many people suffering as we do. There is just so much that they could do, the rest is up to you. Don't get into a state of FEAR; False Evidence Appearing Real. Society uses fear-based tactics, that if you don't do it their way, you're doomed. That is such false propaganda. God is the almighty power and God is within you. No one has the authority to pass a judgement of how long you have to live, or the quality of your life, if you don't do a certain procedure or take certain medications. I was told I would be in a wheelchair if I didn't do a certain operation. My body actually built a bridge where they were supposed to put a pin. There are what seem to be miracles every day. The truth is, "the Power within

You is Greater than any Circumstance Around You." You and God within have total dominion over those thoughts and actions, which will bring you the results you want. Feed your fear or feed your faith; it's always your choice. Feed your Faith!

There is no substitution for water! You have ignored your body's cry for water. Instead, you drink caffeinated, carbonated, alcoholic, and dietary beverages that cause more dehydration and acidosis. Coffee, beer, and alcoholic beverages cause dehydration. If you are drinking these, you need double the amount of water to stay properly hydrated. Good hydration is the foundation of good health.

"More than 2 Million Americans become seriously ill every year because of toxic reactions to correctly prescribed medicines taken properly" . . . Washington Post. The article states it is the fourth most common cause of death in the country. Drink more water! You can't depend on meds to do all the work. *"The extra water you drink when you take a pill does more good than the pill"*. . . . Darrell J Stoddard

Your symptoms of a water shortage are: constantly feeling tired without doing physical work; having the feeling of not wanting to get out of bed; having anxiety, agitation, phobias, shortness of temper, depression, sleep disorders, or cravings for sodas, alcohol, and hard drugs. These are all cries that there is a water shortage, the body is not in balance, and is looking for a temporary fix that leads to more dehydration and a vicious cycle. How could you stop the cycle? Start your morning off with 16 oz. of fresh, clean water to flush out your digestive tract and rehydrate your system from the overnight fast. Drink about 4 oz. every hour to help keep up mental activity. If you are perspiring a lot from exercise or external activity, make sure you rehydrate. Sweat cleans the lymphatic system and the bloodstream, so keep hydrated. Thirty minutes before each meal, have minimal 8-16 oz.; this gets your digestive enzymes going and helps clean the tract. Drink at least an 8-oz. glass of water before bed; it keeps the heart pumping. Many hearts stop during the night due to dehydration—the heart is a pump—the pump needs water; water is the conduit. Without water, the heart can't keep doing its job. Having the glass of water before bed is very important. Many elders don't want to drink before bed because they don't want to go to the bathroom at night. As you start drinking more and more, your bladder will get stronger and stronger as you flush out the acid waste. Many medications have weakened your bladder.

Water to the body, is like what gas is to a car. If the tank is full, it keeps running; when you run out of gas, or you run out of water, it just stops. The energy from the conduit just stops. We are energy and need water to keep it fueled. Water empowers the body's natural healing process.

Your body's reactions to a drought are: allergies, asthma, hypertension, type 2 diabetes, and autoimmune disease. Complications of dehydration include obesity, hemorrhoids, cholesterol plaques, arterial diseases, type 1 diabetes, and serious neurological disorders such as Alzheimer's disease and Parkinson's disease. Multiple sclerosis, neuritis, phlebitis, lymphomas, cancer, and many more distinct names of dis/eases that the medical industry puts a label on, are very much connected to dehydration. What they are not aware of is that many of these conditions are caused by prolonged chronic dehydration and could start to clear up once the body becomes well and regularly hydrated with the essential mineral water and a 1/2 tsp. of sea salt. Increased water intake increased bone density by 10–17%.

Like anything, too much of a good thing is *not* recommended. Do not think that you could reverse dehydration by drinking it all at once? *Do not* drink more than 80 ounces in one hour. Space it out because you don't want to put too much energy in at one time. It will cause a short and an imbalance, and it will cause many complications. Your organs are not meant to handle too much of anything in a short period of time. That rule is for eating and drinking. Don't overload your organs; respect your kingdom.

Water is the most inexpensive, non-invasive, healthiest way to take care of your body. Proper intake transports nutrients, removes waste, flushes toxins, improves oxygen, facilitates breathing, lubricates joints, absorbs shock in joints, regulates temperature, helps you heal faster, look better, gives you more energy, helps you think clearer, helps you see clearer, sleep better, helps allergies, helps asthma, and much, much more. As a child, I had severe asthma. I really didn't drink any water. I drank a lot of milk. Which at the time I didn't know, caused a lot of inflammation. I started to get rid of my asthma when I joined a gym at 13 years old and started exercising and bringing water to drink. I didn't realize this important link, back then. I think this is very important information to save another child who is not drinking water and is suffering for their life with asthma. Awareness needs to be brought to the schools on the importance of water. Water awareness needs to be brought to everyone.

The next best thing, if you or someone you love doesn't like to drink water because they don't want to go the bathroom, is to let them soak in either an Epsom salt or Baking Soda bath. An Epsom salt bath is used to open your lymph flow and blood circulation by alkalizing and warming the tissues of the body. Baking Soda baths are relaxing and soothing to the body, also. Water is a great stress reducer. A warm bath before bed is great for relieving the stress that causes insomnia. Our skin is the largest organ of our bodies so, if the body is severely dehydrated, it will soak it up. Use a few drops of essential oils like peppermint or lavender for soothing effects; don't use chemically made bubble bath.

Water helps nourish and cleanse your Pineal Gland, which is located a little above the center of your eye brows. This small little gland is your main connector to your Universal Intelligence within. When it is not calcified, you see things clearer and have better intuition. It is your life energy connector, your link to the infinite. When blocked, you lose your connection to your higher power. In the next chapter, I am going to speak about a water that brings your life energy even higher because it helps decalcify your pineal gland that has gotten calcified from too much fluoride in the drinking water and the tooth paste. Society doesn't even realize that they are becoming foggy brained and more dependent on others. You need to open up your third eye so you can see things clearer and you can start designing the life you want to live.

Let's reiterate the Royal Flush: Ace for your Heart is Love; King for your Heart is Oxygen; Queen for your Heart is Water; Jack for your Heart is Enzymes; and the 10 for your Heart is Exercise. Do you like my analogy? Hope it makes it easy for you to remember.

So I was able to amp up your power with the knowledge of drinking more water. In the next chapter, I want to amp up your knowledge of a water that will amp up your power even higher, I call it—"God's living water," so do many others.

POWER PAGE . . . AMP UP YOUR POWER!

(Write Your Thoughts, Words and Affirmations)

_____

_____

_____

_____

_____

_____

_____

_____

_____

_____

_____

_____

_____

_____

_____

_____

_____

_____

_____

_____

_____

CHAPTER 7

THE POWER OF DRINKING IONIZED, ALKALINE WATER

What is Ionized, Alkaline water? In simple terms, it is super charged micro clustered water. It makes you feel good, look good and gives you more energy. It is one of the highest antioxidants you could put into your body to fight free radical damage and it's only water. I have been drinking Ionized alkaline water for over 6 years and it is my favorite appliance in my kitchen. I wouldn't trade it for any amount of money because of the benefits it has brought me.

There are many ionizers on the market, just do your homework before purchasing. Make sure they are made with medical grade titanium platinum plates. You need special plates to be able to handle the amount of electricity that is splitting the water during the electrolysis process, into the negative and positive ions. I am grateful there are many companies trying to share the same message, just be a smart consumer, many use metal and mesh plates and after a few years could break down and go into the water, also choose one that has a constant energy supply, not switch mode, for higher efficiency.

The ionizer that I own is "Kangen" by Enagic. I call Kangen, *God's living water*. Kangen means: *Back to the Origin*. God intended you to drink the water fresh from the mountains and the streams, being alive and full of energy. Enagic was able to simulate the water God put on the earth. Fresh from the mountains and the glaciers is best, Kangen is the next best water, in my opinion. It is the Queen energy for your heart; it really amps up your power and gives you much more clarity to your higher self.

The benefits of negative ions were first studied by the Russians in the mid-1800s. They found negative ions to be the missing link in damaged cells. Negative ions are an important building block to the human body for repair and to restore free radical damage. Russia invented the first water ionizers in the early 1900s. In the 1950s, Japan looked into making ionizers for commercial use. They started experimenting on plants and animals, and it was determined that it was very safe and successful. Japan made the first residential water ionizer in 1958. In the 1960s, the Soviet Union established the Chelyabinsk Project to determine if ionized water could remove radiation from the body. Many people had been exposed to radiation during nuclear research and development at the time of the Cold War. It was determined that the water effectively helped detox the heavy metals and kept the cells properly hydrated. In 1966, the Japanese Health Ministry approved the water ionizer as a *Health Improving Medical Device.* Korea followed suit and approved the water ionizer as a medical device, 10 years later. It is still in their hospitals today. They use both the negative ions and positive ions to help restore the body and for sanitation purposes. The 2.5, which is a positive ion, is used as an antibacterial and kills the following: staph, mercer, gangrene, pink eye, viruses, and helps bed sores. It also sterilizes equipment. It is not harmful in any way for you, but it kills or retards growth of bacteria on contact. The 8-11.5 is known as the negative ions; this water is anti-inflammatory, helps with inflammation, acid reflux, IBS, and any other inflammatory dis/eases. It helps bring the body to homeostasis (balance) with no side effects. This is such important information to reach the public; there are too many naysayers that can't believe something so simple could make such a difference. I just recommend that you *try* the water—what do you have to lose? . . . except toxins. For more information go to:

FeelGreatwithWater.com

FeelGreatwithWater.info

"Drinking the right water, not just any water, is critical for your health and prevention of disease. This is true, now more than ever, in our acidic 21st century society."

—Horst S. Filtzer, MD, F.A.C.S.
Former Chief of Surgery,
Cambridge Hospital,
Harvard Medical School.

All waters are not created equal. Just like there are different gases that you put into your car, you wouldn't put regular gas into your Ferrari, so why would you put regular water into your engine that is powering you? What you put in affects every one of the trillion cells in your body. You run on water, not coffee. God knows I am always searching for the best for my body. That being said, I feel I was guided to the best drinking water, I am very grateful and I just want to share my knowledge. "You can lead a horse to water, but you can't make the horse drink it." That reminds me of a friend of mine that gave her horse the water—he knows the difference and only drinks Kangen now. They say horses are very smart animals.

Not only is Ionized water one of the best drinking water, it is one of the best substance you could put into your body. It is a powerful antioxidant: it alkalizes; it hydrates; it detoxifies every cell in your body. The Ionizer sits next to your sink. It either gets hooked to your faucet or gets directly connected to your cold water line. It takes your regular tap water, goes through a carbon filter, and then goes through 3–8 medical grade titanium platinum plates, depending on the unit you purchase. The water goes through an electrolysis process, which splits the regular H20 into -0H and +H ions. The ionizers range from $1480.00-$4980.00. I predict that it will be the next appliance in everyone's home. It's a necessity, not a luxury. Not all ionizers are created equal. If they don't have medical grade titanium plates, I don't consider them an ionizer and I don't consider them safe. That is why I don't recommend using anything but Kangen; I know it's been around for over 40 years. It came to the United States in 2003, starting out in California, came to New York in 2004, and it is now making its way around the globe.

Let me tell you a little story of how I got introduced to Kangen. It was the first week of May 2011. I had called up a friend, Rick to see how things were going. He knew how passionate I was about my health, my family's health, and about helping others with their health. He told me of this new marketable technology from Japan that makes ionized alkaline water. I was pretty impressed because, at the time, I had studied as a holistic health practitioner and everything I learned was about how important it is to alkaline the body, remove acid waste, try to maintain a healthy neutral state, and, of course, water was key. So, I love water, and I know the importance of water. I carried bottled water with me everywhere I went, so this sounded like the answer to my prayers (literally) because I did have some health challenges. I asked how much it would cost. To me, I saw value. I told him, "I want this water; order it right away." I felt it was a necessity, not a luxury. So, being excited, I told my husband what I had just ordered and explained how my friend, Rick, did intense research. I knew he wouldn't just buy something without researching every detail about it; he had the product over 6 months already. Well, when I told Den the price, he didn't have quite the same reaction that I did (lol); he literally picked up the stool nearby, and he looked like he was going to hit me with it. He said, "Are you crazy???" I said, "No! You are, you don't know the importance of it!" The funny thing is, the following week they were having a convention in Palm Desert, California, and guess what? It was our 25th anniversary, May 17th, so I talked him into going to Palm Desert for 6 days for our anniversary. He liked the idea, so off to California we went. He really was enjoying the convention. At one point, there was this older woman that stood behind him in line. She mentioned to him she had been drinking the water for over a year. She was stating how she no longer has her arthritic pain in her hands that used to stop her from knitting. Then there was a 72 year old woman that used to be in a wheel chair and is now getting around better than before. I am talking about drinking water—no magic potions and no lotions, it's about being properly hydrated. Den was actually very impressed. The next thing that happened is going to "wow" you, I still can't believe it happened. At one point during the event, they were raffling a machine. I didn't purchase any tickets. Den had gone to the men's room. They began the raffle. I started visioning having another machine. At the time, I had a hair salon, so I am visioning giving out gallons to people at my salon, all of a sudden, they called my name to the stage. OMG! I go up there and they ask, "So, how long have you been a distributor?" I respond, "I didn't even get my machine yet." It was in transit as we were on our way to California. The whole audience was laughing and clapping with joy. My face was beaming, and I was so grateful! When Den came back to his seat, he couldn't believe it; he was so amazed and happy. Den said, "As I was on my way to the men's room, I bought 5 raffles, $10 each, and I put your name on them because the one next to me always wins." That was so great because it was like we got 2 for 1, all because I had faith in the process. From that point, I knew for sure I was destined to hand out gallons to bring God's water into every household. It is my passion to educate more and more people about this special water.

The company and I don't make any claims that the water heals anything, when you give the body what it needs, it will heal itself. Water is a big component of healing, especially when you are 75% water, and because it is ionized and micro-clustered, it makes it that much more absorbable.

Since water is a key nutrient next to oxygen, it is important that you put the very best into your God-given body. It's best when you drink it fresh from the mountains or glaziers, it has a natural electrical charge to it and is more alkaline. God created the water on this Earth many centuries ago; now that centuries have passed, our water has changed. The molecules have gotten so big, making it much harder for it to penetrate into your cells. It's like trying to take tennis balls and throwing them against a chain linked fence—some may get in, most don't. Now, take micro-clustered, ionized water; it is like taking marbles and throwing them against the same linked fence—practically every one of them will get in, for much better hydration. You will notice right away in your skin, hair and nails.

Bottled water is lifeless water. It is bottled 12–18 months before you even drink it. It is boiled at 180 degrees before they put into the bottles, causing cancer-causing chemicals to be leached into the bottled water—and you are paying for this? Most bottled waters are very oxidizing. There is a vortex the size of Texas in the middle of the ocean, polluted with billions upon billions of plastic bottles. The plastic particles are going into our food chain. Are you ok with that? I am not! The tap water is city regulated to be neutral, but so many toxic chemicals, like lye, fluoride, and now pharmaceutical drugs, are getting into your water supply. This is not good! Reverse Osmosis is bad for your bones because the water is stripped of minerals and, again, you're drinking lifeless water.

What choices do you have? I am not trying to bring fear into you, I am trying to awaken and educate you, there is a simple answer. Ionized Alkaline Water.

Ionized Water is also known as hexagonal water, reduced water, or ERW. It provides superior hydration, enhanced nutrient absorption, quicker detoxification, increased metabolic efficiency, and improved cellular communication. For more health benefits of ERW water, you could go to pubmed.gov

Osteoporosis was once thought to be a disease of older people. Now, teenagers are beginning to be diagnosed with osteopenia, the beginning stages off osteoporosis; teens are very acidic. When the body becomes acidic from all the sodas, sugary drinks, processed foods, and even dairy products, there is excess acid in the blood, in order to buffer the excess acid in the blood, it will steal calcium from your bones, which will weaken them, making you prone to injury. It takes a special kind of water to bring the body to balance, and I feel, I have found it. I no longer have tennis elbow in my left elbow and no longer have pain in my right knee from years of exercising doing kickboxing, spin and step classes. I was not being properly hydrated, even though I drank a lot of water.

The aging process is a loss of water from your organs, your tissues, and your cells. When there is inflammation around the organs, it is very hard for regular, non-reduced water to get into the cells. When the water is ionized, it becomes micro-clustered, it neutralizes the free radical damage and helps the cells start repairing. Healing for the cells is at a -40 voltage—Kangen ionized water is -300 to -800 voltage. The more you keep drinking, the more cells could start repairing. You are energy, and you need to keep your voltage up. It's science. Many of the *dis/eases* are shortage in the voltage. It is like your neurotransmitters start shorting out.

A very big concern to me is that our babies of today are being born acidic. The acidosis from the moms are being passed down. Pregnant moms should stay away from sugary carbonated drinks, it is too acidic. Babies are supposed to be born slightly more alkaline. They start out are about 90% water. Water is a key essential, is a necessity for their developing brains. Pregnant moms should especially be drinking at least 80 oz a day, minimal. Now, because the molecules of regular water are so big, babies are spitting up too much, so doctors are recommending babies not have water until after six months. This is a huge concern of mine, especially, if the doctors are giving babies shots, while they are in an acidosis stage. A baby's immune system is not strong enough to ward off foreign particles, and water is the key nutrient to get these particles out of the body—if you don't have water, it could be very detrimental for the development of the baby's brain. The reason for the restriction is many babies can't digest the size of the clusters from regular H2O. Kangen puts out -OH (molecular oxygen and molecular hydrogen) which is the highest antioxidant that I have found that is beneficial for the body. It will penetrate into the cells before it even hits the baby's stomach. It will be an asset in brain development. We need to get this info out.

I found that this special water could play a major role for people with Alzheimer's, Dementia, MS, Parkinson's, ADD, ADHD, Autism, Migraines, Insomnia, Depression, Bi-Polar Disorder, and Cancer, as well as any other brain disorders. Each is connected to severe inflammation in the brain. Being severely dehydrated, regular water can't get in because the clusters are too big. By drinking Kangen water, it will help penetrate the blood brain barrier and help reduce the inflammation around the brain. A couple of other great regimens is to orally take a tablespoon of coconut oil, a couple of times a day, and get Copaiba essential oil, drop a couple of drops on your fingertips and place it about an inch above your ears, to help penetrate the brain barrier and help reduce inflammation. Not too many things penetrate the blood brain barrier, but all of these do, and it takes a special water to get through. That is why this message is so important to get out there. Too many people are suffering from brain issues, and inflammation is the silent killer.

Many people are suffering with back and neck pain from herniated discs, also caused by severe inflammation and severe dehydration. The discs start flattening out when they don't get enough water; it takes a special water to get in to neutralize the inflammation and bulk up the jelly in the vertebras.

A really important thing about Kangen is that it helps eliminate acid waste and trapped proteins that are damaging your lymphatic system. When your tissues are filled with acid waste, your cells and tissues become very sensitive to touch. This is a trait in many children with autism. Drinking the ionized water and getting lymphatic massages could help drain the toxins out of the body.

What do you do when you feel sluggish? You might go to the doctor. He might give you a pill, and you might start feeling a little better because you were given something to Band-Aid one of the symptoms of dehydration. When your body is sluggish, it is usually caused by being severally dehydrated, you have acid waste and maybe some trapped protein buildup somewhere. Your organs are working way too hard, and it puts your body in a state of fatigue. If you're not drinking enough water, you could get shut down, like a piece of equipment that got jammed up. Everything becomes stagnant. Water is to the body, like oil is to machinery—it needs it, or it will get rusty and stop working. Ionized water helps clean the rusty pipes, lubricates the joints, and cleans out the rotors.

What do I do, when I feel sluggish? I will go on a one to three-day fast with the ionized water. I will add lemon to the water. I will take my Fruit and Vegetable Enzymes, some Ukon (a product with turmeric) and drink ionized water all day long. I keep flushing; I don't worry about going to the bathroom—I have to get the acid waste out, so my body could function better. Doesn't this make sense? I only go to the doctor for a checkup, once a year, to hear a good bill of health. Before I started drinking Kangen, I had a few issues:

my thyroid was acting up; my heart had a murmur; I was told I was headed towards a stroke; I had some women's issues, a skin condition called melasma, and the start of osteopenia in my bones. My body repaired 90% of it.

When you have a crisis in your body, let the body go into repair mode; let it concentrate on what it needs to fix. Your body wants to stay alive and healthy more than you know; it is well equipped when you give it the "Royal Flush." It does whatever it needs to do to accomplish its mission. When your body is going through a real crisis, try to take in only liquid foods that are easily digested; by feeding the body solid foods, it has to concentrate on digesting food, which takes a lot of energy. When you fast for a couple of days, your body goes into repair. See how you feel in a couple of days. You should feel your body getting better and better. Sometimes you might detox for a day and feel a little worse, that is because the body is purging the wastes out. The key is to keep drinking the water, flushing out the toxins. You will start feeling brand new in a couple of days. You are just giving your organs a little vacation from digesting.

To sum things up, the only water I personally recommend is Kangen Water, which means *Back to the Origin*. The Japanese were able to simulate the next best water the way God intended us to drink it: fresh, clean, and energized clusters for quick absorption into all your cells. Throughout the centuries since

God put the water on our planet, the structure of it has gotten bigger, making it less permeable. In the mid 1800's the Russians were the first to discover importance of why ionized water is so important. In the 1960s, the Soviet Union did a project that showed the ionized water helps get the radiation metal toxicity out of the body. Japan has been drinking ionized water for over 40 years, and they are #1 on the health charts; the United States is #38 and climbing.

Reminder about The Royal Flush: Ace is the Love for your heart; King is the Oxygen for your heart; Queen is the Water for your heart; Jack is the Enzymes for your heart; 10 is the Exercise for your heart. Your heart is the soul of your kingdom—keep it happy.

In this chapter, I showed you how to amp up your power by drinking Ionized Alkaline Water. Now, you are going on to read about the Jack for you heart, which are the enzymes. You will also learn, the importance of essential oils, repair and elimination, and how it revs up your power.

POWER PAGE . . . AMP UP YOUR POWER!

(Write Your Thoughts, Words and Affirmations)

_____

_____

_____

_____

_____

_____

_____

_____

_____

_____

_____

_____

_____

_____

_____

_____

_____

_____

_____

_____

_____

CHAPTER 8

THE POWER OF ENZYMES, OILS, REPAIRING AND ELIMINATION

The Jack for your heart, are the enzymes, one of the royalties for your kingdom. They have a very important role in your kingdom. Live enzymes are what you get from fresh fruits and vegetables. Try to stick to eating 80/20—80 percent whole foods and 20 percent of the other stuff you like to eat. Fruits and vegetables are the living nourishment from the earth that God gave you. Living foods are full of oxygen, water, and enzymes—the three royalties to keep your kingdom powerful.

Your quick paced life looks for fast, easy, convenient ways to feed yourself and your family. You may choose poorer choices because of convenience. Fast food, pre-packed, or microwaved food all have lifeless enzymes. It is considered dead food. Your body needs live enzymes. No live enzymes are in processed, hydrogenated foods. They send out particles that cannot be processed by the body, therefore, get stored in the fat cells or clog up your blood stream, causing the heart to work harder. Switch to eating a more plant based diet. Eating at least 4 fruits and 5 vegetables a day is what is minimally required. It is always best to eat your fruits and vegetables free from herbicides and pesticides, and that is a challenge to find. *"Diseases such as heart disease, stroke, cancer, and diabetes remain leading causes of death and disability in the United States. Substantial scientific research over the past few decades indicates that diet can play an important role in prevention of such conditions."* . . . former U.S. Assistant Secretary of Health. What you put into your body affects the energy that your body produces—keep your body fueled with the right stuff and you will stay amped up. Living enzymes from whole foods is key. Diets that include more vegetables are more alkalizing and can enhance calcium retention in your bones.

I am so grateful I was introduced to a whole food nutritional product that made it simple and easy for my family and I to get the enzymes from fruits and vegetables that we needed. I know, we were not eating enough of them, because of our busy lives. My now lifelong friend, Linda, was taking one of my Pilates classes for the first time, back in 2005. After class, she asked me if I would listen to a cd. I said, "Sure!" She called me a week later, and I told her I still hadn't listened to the cd, but I did promise her I would. That weekend, my family and I were going upstate, and I decided to listen to the cd on the drive up there. I was listening to a doctor that was an oncologist, I was very intrigued with what she was saying about the importance of fruits and vegetables and how the enzymes helped build up the immune system. It was like I just found out about the discovery of the antibiotic, I knew fruits and vegetables were important, but I didn't know how important they were. I was so excited I called Linda up the next day. I told her, "Not only do I want the product, I also want to educate others of the importance of it." My family and I have been taking the fruits and vegetables in capsule since 2005, and I highly recommend supplementing in the enzymes if you are not eating enough fruits and vegetables. In the morning, I take 2 Orchard Blend capsules which provides me with whole-food-based nutrition from apples, oranges, pineapple, cranberries, peaches, papayas, acerola cherries, prunes, dates and beets. Right before lunch or dinner, I take 2 capsules of the Garden Blend, which provides you with enzymes from broccoli, parsley, tomato, carrots, garlic, beets, spinach, cabbage, oat bran, rice bran, and kale. I don't know about you, but I would have a hard time eating all these fruits and vegetables on a daily basis. Enzymes help with digestion and help nourish every one of your trillion cells. The enzymes help keep your immune system strong. I don't remember the last time I was on an antibiotic. Give your royal kingdom the enzymes that it needs and it will stay strong and defeat anything that comes its way. If you're interested in finding out more go to . . . <u>FeelGreat123.com</u>

Are you drinking coffee with any of your nutritional supplements? Not a good idea. You are defeating the purpose, your nutrients are not being absorbed properly. Coffee is very acidic and stops the nutrients from being absorbed properly. Your body absorbs nutrients better when it's above 6.6 pH, that is why I take my supplements with ionized alkaline water.

One of the key ways to maintain your healthy and happy body is to stay slightly alkaline. I have learned this very important detail through all my studies. This is a challenge, because of all the delicious acidic foods that taste good, and you enjoy eating them. Finding foods to keep your body slightly alkaline and that taste good is a little bit of a challenge, also. I am always looking, and it is funny how God puts different things that I am looking for right in front of me. Remember your thoughts and words create your outcomes. Five years ago, I had attended a Wellness/Yoga convention in NYC, and I had come across a booth called SevenPoint2, an Alkalining company. There, I met this lovely, very intelligent, sweet lady, Ilene. We started talking and we really hit it off. Ilene had so much knowledge about the company that I thought it was hers. She went on telling me how her brother Howard, who is a chiropractor in California, and has his own clinic, developed these wonderful products. They are: Alkaline Boosters, Recovery capsules, Greens, and a Vanilla Shake, a plant based protein powder. I tried the products and loved them. I told her I would like to educate others about these products because I find them to be very important. At the time, she was an attorney and now has recently retired. She has her degree in nutrition and is working towards becoming a Naturopathic Doctor. Seven-Point2, the alkaline company, focuses on a few top of the line products that really help neutralize the acid in the body to help the body feel good, look good, and have more energy. I enjoy starting my morning with a nutritious Greens Shake, which is a proprietary blend of organic certified barley grass, wheatgrass, alfalfa leaf, oat grass, parsley, cabbage, dandelion, carrot, kale, spinach, broccoli, and a few other natural ingredients. You would think it would taste like grass, it actually has a nice smooth taste to it. Acid is the culprit to every dis/ease of the body and keeps spreading like a wild fire, unless you alkalize it. Sevenpoint2 has a product called Alkaline Booster, which is a restorative powder in a capsule consisting of sodium bicarbonate, magnesium bicarbonate, potassium bicarbonate, himalayan crystal salt, fennel seed, marshmallow root and organic lemon powder. These are alkalizing minerals, necessary for repair. I take 2 capsules after an acidic meal and before bed. It helps you neutralize the acid in your body, causing you to sleep better, and it aids to help repair throughout the night. Another great product is called Recovery, which is clinically tested to produce molecular hydrogen, I feel it complements the ionized alkaline water I drink; both of which help put out the fire (acid) in the body. It also helps relieve the discomfort (lactic acid) after a workout; I take a couple after I work out. For lunch or when I am on the go, I will make a SevenPoint2 Vanilla Shake; it has 21 grams of organic sprouted brown rice and yellow pea protein, and it tastes like vanilla cake. If you're interested in learning more, go to . . . AlkalineUrBody.com

Why are essential oils so important? Essential oils are nature's pure essence, also known as the quintessence. The four elements are earth, water, fire, and air. The fifth element, or quintessence, is spirit or life force. The oils are known for their life force (spirit). Why do you think the three kings went out of their way to bring gifts of frankincense and myrrh to baby Jesus centuries ago? Those same oils are being used today. They are the healing oils from the bible. They have been the healing remedy for centuries. Essential oils are health promoting botanicals distilled from the leaves, stems, flowers, roots, and bark; they are highly concentrated and are the true essence of the plant. Benefits are usually achieved through methods of inhalation from a diffuser, drops under the tongue, or drops put on different points of the body, either concentrated or diluted. I like to mix with coconut oil. They are readily absorbed by your trillions of cells in moments, having many benefits. The pure substances in the oils stimulate your smelling receptors and activate your brains limbic system that is associated with memory, emotions, and state of being. The essential oils provide valuable psychological and physical therapeutic benefits. On the other hand, drugs and antibiotics are treated as foreign molecules that disrupt your normal functions of your body. With every pro to a drug, there is a con. With essential oils, there are only pros. Drugs clog and confuse receptors and suppress the immune system; oils strengthen the immune system, clean and restore receptor sites, and detoxify. Antibiotics kill good and bad bacteria; oils only attack the harmful bacteria, allowing your bodies own good bacteria to flourish and fight anything that comes its way. Oils address the root cause of dis/ease at a cellular level, reprogramming correct information into yours cells so they function better and are in harmony with each other. I am friends with many doctors, and they say you plead for more and more scripts. You want a quick fix—a magic pill—and it becomes a domino effect, going from one script and adding another and another, while never getting to the root cause, and never getting a complete healing, because drugs don't heal, don't expect them to. I am not knocking the medical industry. For emergency situations, they are a must; but on daily maintenance, you need to get to the root of why your kingdom is not running smoothly. I am shedding light upon the secrets of the ancient healers: they used the earth's essences. There is a very beneficial therapy called *Raindrop* therapy. The oils have an intelligence of knowing what you need. There is nothing that heals you except your own power and your own immune system. Give the body what it needs, and it will take care of itself. If you want to learn more go to . . . <u>FeelGreatwithOils. info</u>

Coconut Oil is known to be anti-bacterial and is one of the great gifts God created for us. Did you ever hear of Oil Pulling? It is very beneficial. What is Oil Pulling? It's not something new, it's been around for over 3,000 years. It's a process where you take a tablespoon of organic virgin coconut oil and you swish it around in your mouth for about 20 minutes. It gets into every nook and cranny. The fatty molecules in the oil attract and bond with the bacteria that shouldn't be there. After 20 minutes, spit out the oil, in a garbage bag, not in the sink (it will clog pipes when it hardens), I learned the hard way . . . lol. It leaves your breath fresher and your teeth whiter. No harmful effects. You could do it daily. Coconut oil also is great for the brain, weight loss and gives you energy. For extra benefits take a tablespoon orally a day. You could add coconut oil to a shake or cook with it.

The best time to repair is while you are sleeping. Many people complain that they don't get good sleep. You need good sleep. Every one of your trillion cells is always in need of repair. Sleep is essential to repair. When you go to sleep, the quality of your sleep is also very important. Make sure you sleep in a non-electronic zone: no computers or cell phones on or near your bed (preferably keep them in another room, if you can). If you can't, keep all electronic devices as far as possible, and no closer than 4 feet. Don't fall asleep with your TV on; put the timer on if you have to. Get into a cleansing routine before bed—brush your teeth, wash your face. A routine right before bed lets your body know it's time to go to sleep. You could have a diffuser on with lavender essential oil; it is very soothing. If you don't have a diffuser, put a drop in the palm of your hand, rub your palms gently together, and then open slightly, keeping them cupped, and bring them around your nose. Take a couple of inhales and exhales. Leave all your fears, doubts, angers, jealousies, and worries outside your bedroom door, and don't pick them up in the morning. When you get under your covers, say your prayers and say thank you for all your blessings in your life. Ask God to keep you and your loved ones healthy, happy, safe, and prosperous. Reflect on your day how you could have been a better person, and then forgive anyone that hurt your feelings that day, and send them prayers and blessings. You are doing this ritual for your own peace of mind. Now, before you drift into a nice sleep, ask the Universe a specific question, one that you need an answer to. Now, go to sleep with complete faith that the power within you is greater than any circumstance around you. "Let go and let God" and drift into a peaceful sleep. You should be getting at least seven hours of sleep at night. I have to admit this is one area where I don't follow my own words. It's not that I can't sleep. I have to say I have a lot of energy and I am always doing something. This is the life I created for myself. I am always looking to accomplish more and more.

Elimination is extremely important. If you don't get the garbage waste out, it just pollutes and intoxicates every organ of your body. You become a backed up garbage disposal, and the outside of your body will be effected by the inside. Your lymphatic system is a critical component to your survival and gets overlooked. It has a major role in maintaining the health of all the connective tissue, which makes up the majority of your body. The sad thing is that it is not looked upon as the root when you are in a state of dis/ease. When your large network of tiny vessels and nodes are not able to efficiently handle the removal of your metabolic waste and excess acid fluids, your cells become congested and don't function properly, causing dis/ease. When your lymphatic system is working properly, it captures the excess proteins that have wandered into the tissues, organs, and the brain, and helps escort them out. Dis/ease begins when fluid stagnates around the cells, creating a very acidosis stage—an environment like a dirty fish tank. When the pH (potential hydrogen) in a fish tank becomes acidic, what happens to the fish? They die, unless you change the water. The same analogy with your body, when your fish tank gets acidic, your organs begin to suffer; they slow down, get sluggish and, eventually, don't work, causing a need of a replacement, or death. The thing is, you could cut out parts, or change parts, but the dirty fish tank is still there. What you need to do, as soon as possible, is start cleaning the fish tank with clean water—not just any water—it needs to be ionized (electrolyze), micro-clustered (quick absorption), and alkaline (8-9.5), to help clean up the dirty fish tank and bring the pH to balance. Your organs work best at neutral, and all bacteria and viruses will die or lay dormant until your body becomes acidic again (hopefully not). Keep your fish tank crystal clear, and your fish (organs and tissues) will stay healthy, happy, and vibrant.

Let's talk about a great way to eliminate; it is through getting a nice massage. If you are sensitive to someone touching you, it is because your tissues and cells are filled with acidic waste. I would suggest you first drink ionized alkaline water to get the acid waste out of your body that is affecting your sensitivity. Then, hopefully you'll be able to enjoy a relaxing massage. Some of the benefits of massage are: it increases blood circulation, relieves pain and stress, relaxes tense muscles, relieves depression and anxiety, speeds the healing process, reduces blood pressure, and builds your immune system. No matter how healthy you are, you still accumulate acid waste and proteins in your body daily. Massage is an important and enjoyable way to keep your cells and tissues free from accumulating waste buildup. Invest in a massage table and have some fun with your partner. Have some aromatherapy going, in a diffuser. Use some coconut oil and a couple of drops of the essential oils. Lavender and peppermint are nice and soothing, yet a refreshing combo to start with. Enjoy!

Women: Let's do the Twist! I know this is going to sound a little bizarre. Twisting the breasts for proper circulation is very important for prevention of dis/ease. After showering take an organic cream, I use a hemp cream; put a little in each hand and go under your breasts with your hands. Now, gently take both of your breasts and twist them 10 times inward and 10 times outward. This is not for pleasure. (lol) The purpose is to bring circulation to the breast area. Cancer likes to settle into fatty tissues that are stagnant, that don't get much oxygen. By gently twisting you are bringing blood filled oxygen into the area, circulating the toxins out, so the body could escort them out of your kingdom. Cancer does not like oxygen, that is a sure sign to get more in. Another great benefit of doing this exercise is, that by gently twisting you are circulating blood to the area, it will keep your breasts firmer.

Keep Moving! Exercising in general is great for circulation and elimination. Pick a few of your favorite ways to exercise and keep up with your regimen. Make sure you drink plenty of water to flush out the lactic acid, the bi-product from exercising.

Some say disease starts in the colon. Whatever comes in, minus the nutrients, should be escorted out within 24 hours. At minimal, you should be having 1–2 bowel movements daily. If you are not, take a look at your royal subjects—are they keeping your kingdom clean and fresh? Look at the Ace for your heart, Love. Are you loving yourself? Fill your heart with love so there is no room for toxic particles. Look at the King for your heart, Oxygen. Are you doing your deep inhaling and deep exhaling? Getting all the toxic, carbon dioxide out? Otherwise, causing you to feel tired and fatigued? The oxygen also helps your bloodstream, and in your organs, move all the sludge out. Look at the Queen for your heart, Water. Like mother earth: 75% water. Are you drinking a minimal of 80 ounces? This is very important because, if you are not getting enough water, you are again not moving the sludge and the acid waste out. Your body toxins become stagnant. If there is not enough water in your organs, your body will distract liquids from your feces to help out one of your organs calling for water; you will become very constipated and very backed up. Drink water! Check the Jack for your heart, Enzymes. Did you eat enough raw fruits and vegetables? The fruits and vegetables bring in more fiber to help move the sludge. The oxygen, water, and the enzymes from the fruits and vegetables, help break down all your food into a more dissolved state, making it easier to be escorted. Last, but not least, check the 10 for your heart, Exercise. To get elimination, moving along quicker, get moving!; you need the key essentials when you are moving, you need more oxygen and water, your body will be calling for them. Don't wait for the body to call—do more deep inhaling, have a big glass of water 10–20 minutes before exercising, and another big glass right after. Problems of elimination will be a thing of the past if you just check your royal subjects first. By taking any over-the-counter medications to make you go to the bathroom, or any diuretics, you are really damaging your own bodies system for elimination, and it will have adverse effects. Your royal subjects hold the key to your royal kingdom, and they will never disappoint you. You OWE it to yourself!

Now let's take a look on how to magnetize money instead of reflecting it away.

POWER PAGE . . . AMP UP YOUR POWER!

(Write Your Thoughts, Words and Affirmations)

_____

_____

_____

_____

_____

_____

_____

_____

_____

_____

_____

_____

_____

_____

_____

_____

_____

_____

_____

_____

_____

_____

CHAPTER 9

THE POWER OF
MAGNETIZING MONEY

I want to raise your vibration to attract more money. How do you achieve that? Just the way you think about money will attract it or retract it. You want to attract it. Let's work on that. I want you to start thinking about money as living currency. Living currency is energy. Money is not just ordinary paper or coins. Like a current, it is circulating freely. Keep the vision that money is like water or electricity—it is always abundantly flowing and the supply is infinite. Written on your money is "In God We Trust." There is such truth in that statement. Trust in God and you will have no fear where your next dollar will come from. One of your biggest concerns is about your money. Money is meant to allow you the freedom to do and be who you were created to be; to bring your gifts to the world and live a happier, healthier more prosperous life.

Are you living in fear, doubt, worry, anger, jealousy, poverty, greed, pain, and suffering? None of these exists with the faith of God. The corrupt of the nation are trying to take God out of the equation. They are trying to create a fear based society, dependent on the government for everything: keeping small, limiting beliefs of lack; creating more hate for one another; taking away the power of the people; taking away the worth of the dollar. I believe God saw this and had to answer your prayers. I believe God sent President Donald J. Trump to be your Savior in this crisis. He is one of the most successful businessmen of your time. Your currency was in jeopardy and was becoming obsolete. President Trump may not have all of the qualifications of a politician, but he has all the qualities that you need right now. President Trump's past is his past. You have the good, the bad, and the ugly; let's move on. He is a regular man that is egotistical. I say that with a lot of respect. I believe and feel it in my heart that Mr. Donald J. Trump was called upon. God does not call the most qualified; he qualifies the call. There is, no saying "No" when God calls upon you. President Trump has a huge mission that he was called upon to serve. He accepted with honor and without pay; he is truly in service. President Trump pledges his allegiance to the flag of the United States of America, under the republic for which it stands, one nation, under God, indivisible with liberty and justice for all. God is the almighty—don't mess with him or anyone in service for him. There will be some rumbling; we must all stay in faith. President Trump is an optimist visionary and sees our great nation as it will be. He knows how to master money. His ego is his asset; he will not let you down. He will raise the nation in glory! Stay strong, stay united, and stay at peace, we will prosper as one nation under God. We will be a reflection for the rest of the world. Your kingdom, your power, and your glory, are all yours now and forever; don't let anyone take that away.

Money is energy and flows abundantly in exchange for other energy. It is constantly flowing from one hand to another. Money is an exchange for services or goods. If you want more energy, you need to give more energy out. You have to fuel the energy; when you see the flame going low, you need to put more wood into the fire before you receive the heat and the energy. If you want more money, you need to find a way to provide more services or goods (legally).

The question is: How do you look at money? Do you see money as the root of all evil? Do you have any other negative describing words for money? If you think or say this about money, money will be reflected away. Your body sets a vibration to push evil away. Your body's energy is resisting evil coming its way, so if money is associated with evil, do you think money is going to come to you? If it does, it won't stay long; money won't feel welcome. Money is far from evil. The lack and fear of not having money is evil. The selfishness and greed of many is evil. The sad thing is people hurt or kill others to achieve money. Money should never be fought for; there is an abundance for everyone. Money itself is not evil; it is your thoughts and words that you are thinking or saying that may be evil. From this day forward, if you haven't already, I want you to look at money with great respect and great honor. I want you to love money and be grateful for money. Start treating money the way you want to be treated. It responds to your thoughts and feelings. Believe it or not, you are either attracting money or sending it away. What is holding you back from manifesting abundance? It could be karma from your thoughts, words and actions. Your perception makes all the difference—it is purely energy.

How do you perceive people that have money? Do you think negatively about people that have money? Are you jealous, bitter, and envious? If so, you are sending a negative vibration to the Universe, that you don't want to be like them. If you want more money, you should associate yourself with people that know how to attract money. You have to start acting like people that have money. Pretend I hired you for a screen play, for the part of a successful executive. Become that person, how would you speak? How would you dress? How would you act? When performing you have to become someone that you're not. Start dressing for success, paying attention how you are speaking and how you are acting. Creating a life that you truly want to live is very similar to acting. First you have to vision, then try it on for size. You have to create an energy tone that is in alignment of what you want. For this vision you want money flowing. What would be your next step to create money flowing from that person you are visioning? Ideas will start to coming to you. You have to be in service to create money. Keep the vision of what you want and come from that visioning daily. Soon energy will start shifting in the direction of your dream. Have patience and trust the process.

How is money flowing in your life? Are you constantly saying, "I don't have money?" "I can't afford . . . ," Stop saying those words! They block your blessings. You should be looking at money with honor and respect because it will bring you blessings. Have gratitude for every dollar that comes in. Say, "Thank you," to everyone that puts money into your hands. Never turn down any money that someone is putting into your hands. Accept all gifts and tips with gratitude; say "Thank you very much!" That is an invitation for more blessings. I learned that message from a spiritual worker that did Reiki at my salon. She told all of us this message, we didn't like to take tips from each other. She said, "it was necessary to receive the money gratefully." It made a lot of sense, so we all did it. Things started shifting more abundantly. Knowing what I know now, everything is energy, and it needs to be an exchange. When you give out services that help the Universe, you will get back one way or another, and you must always remain in gratitude. Gratitude is the magnet to more money. Gratitude is the magnet for amplifying more of everything. Put Gratitude in your Attitude morning, noon and night!

Let's change things up, if you are not doing this already. You are going to respect yourself first. You are going to respect all others—not just some people— All! You are going to forgive all your enemies. You don't have to do it verbally, just in your mind and soul. Your body will release the tension that is stored somewhere. You are going to respect money and be grateful for every dollar that comes into your hands. You are only going to put your energy on positive thoughts; when a negative one comes along, change the channel or cancel/delete the thought. You are only going to say respectful things about yourself, others, and money. Let your actions be a reflection of what you want. Universal law: Don't do to others what you don't like done to yourself.

You are a master creator, and money allows you to bring your invisible thoughts into visible, physical matter. The sky is the limit. Money has tremendous power and energy to bring you, into the life you see yourself living. Stay in service, keep moving, and doing, while you keep visioning and creating. Your life is forever seeking more. There is an attitude that you have to maintain every step of the way. At every step you need to be happy and keep the faith of knowing you will keep receiving more and more. The enemy of *happy* is *fear, doubt, and worry*. They will keep you unhappy. Once you let fear, doubt, or worry take over, it shuts all your blessings. Your body goes into a pity party, and you start magnetizing all the negative crap your way. Then you wonder, "Why me?" Think about how many times you say: I don't have the money; I am broke; I can't afford it; it's too much money; I am poor; I have bad luck; Nobody cares about me; and many other phrases that you say daily. Cancel/Delete! I want you to pretend, each time you are thinking or saying these words, that you are typing them into a computer. Instead of the internet, you are connected to the infinite, and it will give you all the results you are typing in. Take another look at those phrases. Is that what you want to own into your life? Think about the phrases you say daily. Record your conversations. Listen to what you are saying. Start correcting what you say. *Say what you want, and really want what you say.* "I have money flowing in all the time. I always have more than enough money. Money works for me."

An ideal vision is to have money keep working for you. Money never tires and has such high energy. The key to generate money is to first find something that will help the many, and in doing so it will generate money to help you. Use your thinking capabilities first. Napoleon Hill didn't write a book titled *Work and Grow Rich*. No, he wrote a book titled *Think and Grow Rich*. It is your thinking that creates for you. I highly recommend you read that book.

One of the richest men in the world, Andrew Carnegie, wanted to conduct an experiment, and he interviewed Napoleon Hill for this task. He asked Napoleon, "Would you be willing to take the next 20 years without pay, and interview all the richest people in the world, find out all their secrets, and put this information into a book so that all people would benefit, and the rich wouldn't die with their secrets inside them?" Napoleon thought about it. In less than 2 minutes, he agreed on performing this large, 20-year project. As of today, over 15 million copies have been sold worldwide. It all started out with a thought that Andrew Carnegie had in his mind. What thought do you have in your mind that could help the many?

Napoleon Hill set out to accomplish Andrew Carnegie's vision. He interviewed over five hundred of the most successful, affluent men and women of his time. Many started in poverty. With putting in much of his time and energy, he uncovered the secrets to great wealth and became wealthy himself. After interviewing with them all, he noticed they all had common thinking amongst themselves. It was the way they all thought that created their wealth. It's a thinking power. If you want to change your results, you have to start thinking correctly. Don't ever let anyone do your thinking. You are a master creator. Own up to it—everything is in the palm of your thoughts.

Get a Vision; try it on for size. (Make adjustments.)

Does it bring you happiness? (Feel your longings and discontents.)

Does it bring happiness to others? (It can't be a selfish vision, that would make others unhappy.)

Identify an exact amount of money that will help you obtain your vision. (Be specific.)

Identify that you need help from your Infinite Source of Power, that is within you.

Identity what you could do right now, with what you have at this point. (Make a list.)

Get a clear vision daily.

State what you want daily.

Take a step with confidence. (You don't have to have the whole road map before you start.)

What is sad is that the power of money is not taught in school. Andrew Carnegie was hoping it would have been. I feel it is very important to get the message out into the schools as early as pre-k. The awareness of the power of your thoughts and words could help transform our planet into a healthier, happier, more prosperous way of living. It will build confidence knowing that your success is not determined by your level of education and your grades. It is so sad, if you consider yourself a failure, if you are academically challenged. You have so many gifts inside you, and you shouldn't allow a piece of paper determine your success. Desire is the key. Many people that didn't graduate went on to be very successful. I am not saying education is not necessary. Knowledge is power; the power of knowing something inside you is greater than any circumstance around you. If you have the desire to do something, you will.

I learned at an early age the value, the self-worth, and energy of money. It is such a great feeling when you can take care of yourself, with your own money. I was grateful that I was brought up learning the value and respect of a dollar. I saw my dad's work ethics. Working two jobs, supporting the family household of 6, he always managed to take care of everything. My mom started going to work when I was around nine, when my youngest brother Eddie started kindergarten. She started pressing clothes at a local dry cleaners to make extra spending money for the family. Dad always let her keep her money to do whatever she wanted to, she ended up spending it on us anyway. I never wanted to ask my mom or dad for money; I saw they worked hard for it. I thought it must be nice to make my own money and do and buy whatever I wanted. So, I started thinking, "How could I make my own money?" At around 12-years-old, I started selling for a company called Cheerful House; it was a mail order company. I sold cards, candles, and other small items to neighbors and relatives. I was a young entrepreneur, and it felt good. I started buying my own clothes and shoes, and I loved going roller skating and to the movies, which I paid for on my own. I even started babysitting so I could earn more money, $1 an hour. Dollars do add up. Start where you are and start with something. I even started making enough money to buy my family birthday and Christmas gifts. That felt really good. I learned the great feeling of independence at a very young age, and I believe this is a key secret to happiness. You build a certain confidence inside you, and I was able to do that with the love and support of my family, and I knew there was a strong power within me. God wants you to have that confidence in yourself; he wants you to create your own independence—he will provide you with all the tools you need, when you believe and walk with him in faith.

Dependency on someone else taking care of you, diminishes your power; it also puts your whole being in a state of dis/ease—mentally, physically, and emotionally. You are meant to take care of yourself, when you don't, your body, mind, and soul don't feel right. If you are staying home collecting, and you are really able to go out there and do something, awaken! Start doing something! The money you receive is not worth trading your life for. You are not truly living. You may be thinking, "If I go to work, I'll make less than this." Not so. The getting paid aspect of working is one thing, but the social, fun, loving experiences are at times so much more life giving that you can't put a price on it. It's your life; it's all your experiences together, that make you who you are today. If you don't have experiences, you will be a nobody in the world—change that up! Your body, your mind, and your soul are yearning for more. You do have a soul purpose, awaken, learn to listen to that small voice speaking. Take a step, sometimes it takes many steps until you understand where you are going. Just keep a vision of what you want.

I remember one of my first real jobs at sixteen years old was working at South Nassau Hospital, the place where I was born. I worked in the dietary department. I used to deliver food trays to patients or work in the cafeteria and serve the doctors their meals, both having a lot of interactions with people, and I made new friends. While I was working part time, after school and weekends, I was going full time to school. I went part time to BOCES for my Cosmetology license, and part time to school for my diploma, so I was working on my skills. Like Jim Rohn says, *"Always work on your skills; they will always bring* you *your money."* From that job, I became a cashier at a local food store. It was a nice experience. I felt the energy flow of money hand to hand, bagging of food, and sharing smiles and interactions with people. Then I went on to work at a bank, while going to college for a one year word processing certificate. While doing that, I also taught a few classes of exercise at Lucille Roberts so I could get my exercise in and get paid at the same time. I did haircuts, and I sold jewelry. I was quite a busy girl; no grass grew under my feet. I even had to juggle seeing my boyfriend from Brooklyn, who is my husband now for 31 years. We saw each other 1–2 times a week. He always made a joke about me living within 20 miles from him. Any more than that, he said he wouldn't have come to see me. That would have been his big loss . . . lol. I really enjoyed being in service and making money, and being around people. I was a good saver; by the time I was 21, I had saved up $25,000. I don't say that to impress you; I say it to impress upon you that those $1's add up. I knew that I wanted to save up for my future, and I took that money along with my husband's $35,000 and we put it on a two-family home. That was such a great accomplishment at that young age, and it felt great.

Before you start buying liabilities, things that cost you monthly, buy assets that could bring you money. Invest in a network marketing company with very low start up, where you are your own boss. If you want to get paid, it's all up to you. I am involved in a few of them. I only get involved in things I believe in. It has to feel right to you, before you try to educate others on it. Don't try to sell anyone anything. No one likes to be sold on anything; they have to find value in a purchase, and it has to feel good and feel right. Having an in-home business also has a lot of tax benefits that you could ask your accountant about. If you don't do well, it's a deduction, but you don't want that as your aim. You can't blame a successful network marketing company if you're not showing up to work daily in your own home. Take out set hours that you are going to work on it and focus on your goals. Real estate is also a good way to build your assets. Start with a two-family home, one that is going to help you build equity. Otherwise, real estate could become a liability. When you build up the equity in the home, don't take out the equity and buy liabilities yet. Take out the equity and buy more real estate that will bring you more equity. My dad showed me how you could start with nothing and keep building. Now that he is retired, his assets work for him. I am following his same footsteps. I am grateful for observing his knowledge.

You have to keep your visions going to create more and more. Never stop dreaming at any age. Your goal is to be better, healthier, wiser, and more abundant than your parents. Don't stay stagnant in the feeling that it's good enough. Your body will show signs of dis/ease, when you should be longing and expanding for more. You'll get growing pains. I believe I felt them at around 37 years old. Listen to your higher power for guidance. Don't have fears, doubts, or worries. I am not saying don't walk with caution; I am saying *walk in faith*. You will learn to resist something when it is not right. Sleep on any big decisions. Your guide knows best. You have to have a lot of patience with the process; it's not a get rich quick, overnight process; although, when in service, it could feel that way. Stay away from making money quick, easy, and unethically. Suing others for false claims is not ethical; it may seem like a good way to make quick money, but it won't be beneficial in the long run. If you are hurting anyone else to gain your fortune, your fortune won't last, different aspects of your life will suffer. Start working with the laws of the Universe, and your life will become balanced, full of abundance, and peaceful. Life is not meant to be difficult—you make it difficult. Life is as fun, easy, and effortless as you make it; it is your perception on how you look at things.

If you don't know where to start, quiet yourself down, and ask your inner self for guidance. You could ask God before you go to bed: "How could I make $$$$ a week to start (whatever amount you want)?" Be very specific. You may not get a direct answer, but just learn to go with the flow. Things will come to you. Sometimes it's not exactly what you are looking for—it's a stepping stone to something better. The important thing is take the step that is in front of you; you don't need to see where it leads to.

Remember where you came from. You have royal blood running through you. God, your father, the almighty maker of the Universe, created you in his likeness. We are all God's children, and heirs to his infinite wealth. Even Jesus had a treasurer. Money is one of the most spoken about in the bible, there was never any lack of anything. God has infinite riches, enough to make every man on earth a millionaire and still have plenty left over. You need to create a millionaire mindset. Surround yourself with people with a positive mindset.

Money can't buy respect, love, family, friends, or happiness. Just because you have money does not mean you are rich. You may have money, but you may suffer with poor health, poor relationships, and poor time freedom. You may have money, but you are not living. If your blessings are not flowing, and your faucet feels dry, I want you to make a checklist of all your fears, doubts, and worries. Read your fears, doubts, and worries and then crumple them up and know with confidence and faith that the power within in you (God) is greater than any of those fears, doubts, or worries. Shut off the energy that you have been feeding those negative feelings and thoughts. Those negative thoughts are blocking your blessings. I want you to put all your energy into knowing that the power within you (God) will magnetize all that you will need. He will sell his cattle for you if you believe in Him and the Power within you. You will never be in lack again. Don't look to others for handouts. You have all the answers within yourself. Work with what you have, and you have much more than you know. The questions you ask God before you go to bed will determine your life. Take the time to ask for what you want, but the key is to be very specific. When it comes to money, be very specific. How much do you want to earn daily, weekly, or monthly? Keep it as a main focus daily. At the same time, you need to be in service.

Everything is an exchange—a giving and a receiving. It is a Universal law. Pretend God is your employer. Think about the planet; think about the people; think about what you don't like; think about what you do like. What would you like to see be changed? What would you like to see embellished? Or, what great gift do you think would help benefit the many? God can't actually do the work himself, so he depends on you and I. God works through you. When you find something that helps all his children, he helps you even more. He will give you all the tools, the money, the energy, and the man power, when you have a great idea. God will give you what you need, and want, when you accomplish what he needs and wants. The more you share your skills, the more you will be blessed and receive. You may be having a pity party right now thinking that you don't have any skills. Yes, you do. God doesn't create junk! You have many gifts, that can bring you money, for the exchange of your service. Keep touching lives. The more lives you touch, the more blessings you will receive. The rewards and the energy that you receive from God does not always have to be money. It could be better health, more loving relationships, a career that you love, more time, more freedom and, better yet, all of these and more.

Be in service, money and blessings will always flow unto you. Walk in Faith into the next chapter.

POWER PAGE . . . AMP UP YOUR POWER!

(Write Your Thoughts, Words and Affirmations)

_____

_____

_____

_____

_____

_____

_____

_____

_____

_____

_____

_____

_____

_____

_____

_____

_____

_____

_____

_____

_____

_____

CHAPTER 10

THE POWER OF
YOUR FAITH AND TRUST

"You will not be Forgotten."

God does not forget any of you. The truth is you may have forgotten about the power of God within you. You are blessed with full dominion over your life. A life full of great health, happiness and prosperity. When you walk in complete faith and trust, you walk with God. You walk with the wisdom and the knowing that you are never alone. You don't dwell on your fears, your doubts, or your worries. You release all jealousy; you forgive those that have hurt you; you turn the other cheek; and you look at the good in everyone, when you walk in faith with God.

You will understand and believe in your own power when you trust in yourself. You need to understand it's not just you alone, ever. You are connected to the almighty God, the maker of heaven and earth, everything visible and invisible, everything you can see and everything you can't see. You have the power of the Infinite. Just because you can't see it, doesn't mean it doesn't exist. Just because it is not in the physical, and your five senses can't pick up on it, you can't feel it, you can't see it, you can't taste it, you can't hear it, or you can't smell it, does not mean it does not exist. That is very small, limiting, low vibrational thinking, and will keep you feeling like you are missing something. You will keep trying to fill the void throughout your life. When you awaken the Holy Spirit that has been in you all along, you will become the master creator yourself. You will no longer have pity parties. You will no longer live in lack. You will no longer have anxiety. You will no longer have depression. You will no longer have dis/ease within yourself. You will no longer have an addiction to anything. You will no longer have to fill that empty void, when you have the faith and trust in yourself, knowing the same power that was in Jesus is the same power that is in you. This was the message then, and this is the message now. You don't need to depend on anyone else but yourself; the answer is within your heart. Awaken the power of your heart with love. Love is the key to your faith and trust in yourself. Believe in you!

God is with you for the small tasks, the large tasks, and the impossible tasks. This reminds me of a little story I want to share. A few years ago, my dad went to the doctor because he was in pain; his shoulder was hurting him. He always lifted heavy things, and nothing ever stopped him from doing what he wanted to do. The doctor checked him and took an x-ray. A few days later, the doctor reviewed the X-ray and told him what he saw and recommended. The doctor told my dad that the x-ray showed bone on bone, and that he wouldn't be able to use his arm anymore the way he used to. When I saw my dad upstate, he looked like he had just lost his best friend. My father was so down and depressed, I asked my dad, "What's the matter?" He was saying how he is useless and he can't do what he used do. When my dad told me this, I was furious that the doctor had told him this because it put my dad in a state of depression. He didn't want to live anymore if he couldn't do what he was used to doing. Yes, in the physical, what the doctor saw was bone on bone; his diagnosis was correct. But the prognosis was not correct to tell my father it would never get better. I don't believe anyone has the right to tell anyone a prognosis (a prediction of a dis/ease); they are not God. I told my dad that he has full dominion over prognosis, and not to let anyone outside of yourself tell you what your end result is, I know my dad didn't really believe me. I told him that the doctor told me I needed a pin in my back, when I was 37 years old, or I was going to be in a wheelchair. I didn't listen and here I am today, pain free! *Refute what you don't want;* and I told this to my dad, but my dad had more faith in the man with the white coat than he did in himself. Who am I? I don't have a PHD. I am just his daughter. Who is he going to listen to? I knew my dad was not taking care of his kingdom with the *Royal Flush* (love, oxygen, water, enzymes, and exercise). I kept on top of my dad trying to get him to drink more water, go swimming, go rowing, and just keep doing. Last summer I said to my dad, "How are things going?" He said, "I'm doing the possible, but the impossible just takes me a little longer." That remark put such a big smile on my face and a warm feeling in my heart. I said, "Thank you, God." With God, nothing is impossible; all things are possible. You will gain full access to your power when you know with conviction that this is truth.

In March of 2014 I was guided to become a Dream Builder coach, that has brought me great confidence and the clarity in my purpose to help others. In October of 2015, God guided me to become ordained by Lightwing Center through LifeSpirit CC to become an Ordained Minister Practitioner of Inspirational Healing Center. It didn't change my faith as a Christian; it actually awakened me more to my Life Spirit within myself. It is not about religion; it about the helping people awaken and connect to their spirit within. Everyone has spirit and we are all connected as one. While writing this book I feel the need to bring God, Love and Light into everyone's hearts. Help you change your mindset and help you amp up the power within your kingdom. To help to strive and keep your kingdom healthy, happy and prosperous. I feel I need to teach the principles of this book. The proceeds from the book will help the mission of the ministry. I feel people are looking for more. This will fill the void. We are all one with God, sharing love and light, this message is needed to be shared. We are all one with Universal Intelligence, the Infinite. When you live in the spirit, there is no pain, no suffering, no dis/ease, no poverty. I am a loyal servant of the lord, my God. I am here to fulfill my promise I made when I was nine years old. When I was struggling for my next breath, I told God, "Help me breathe, and I will help you." God helps me daily to fulfill my needs and wants. Now I am here to serve him to help you fulfill all your needs and wants. "Thy Will be done!"

We live in a metaphysical world. Everything is created twice. If you think it, you could create it. You could "Will it" into existence. When you "Will" something, the Universe thinks you desire it, and will do anything it can to bring it into existence. As I said in the chapters I wrote earlier, your thoughts, words, and actions have power. Pay attention and be careful what you are "Willing" into existence. God gave you full dominion of your thoughts. If you think sickness, disease, pain, suffering, or poverty, you will "Will it" into existence. I want you to start Willing what you want. Have the power in Faith. Will into existence good health, happiness and prosperity. What is it that you want? If you think about something so much, make sure you want it. You have complete dominion over your life. If your life is not going right, you have no one to blame except yourself. Having faith is not about religion or being religious. Having faith is having a complete confidence, knowing the power within you is greater than any circumstance around you. God does not Will pain, sickness, or poverty onto anyone. That is not God's Will. That is man-made through karma, words, thoughts, and actions.

It is said that we pick our parents; either we need to teach them a lesson, or they need to teach us a lesson. We are here to create a Heaven on Earth. It may not be Heaven on Earth right now, but you cannot control how others are thinking, feeling, or what they are doing. You can only take care of your own kingdom, and guide those in need to connect to their higher self. Stay in service to carry the light and help awaken others that may be sleeping or are in darkness. Don't let what is going on around you get inside you. You are here not to follow past generations; you are here to be better than your ancestors. You are evolving to better and better technology, better health, more happiness, and more prosperity. You have to keep going forward and upward. When something is out of your control, walk forward in faith, and don't look back. Do not judge others. Do not tell others what they need to do. Guide others to their own power that is within themselves. Their own higher self, which is connected to the infinite, will guide them in any circumstance. Your soul purpose is to be in service to others and guide and awaken yourself. Take control of your own words, thoughts, and actions—be sinless.

At times, it could become very challenging for you, watching loved ones, family, and friends that are in darkness and have not awakened their power. The only thing you can do is pray for them and send them love and blessings. Keep the vision for them that they will get through their challenges. Tell them that you believe in them, and they should have confidence in believing in your belief. Two or more people praying and believing on something really gives it more power and energy. Keep love in your heart and send them blessings of health, happiness, prosperity, and safety.

At a very young age, I started going to church with my noni, my dad's mom, who lived upstairs from us. I always loved church. I liked sitting in the front row (I still always like sitting in the front row), and I loved the feeling that I felt afterwards.

At around the age of sixteen, I was going less and less to church. There came a time that I thought, "I don't need to go to church because God is always with me at all times." I felt very secure with my faith. I started creating the life I wanted: I got married; I created a home; I had my three children, and I took them to church (just for CCD purposes and on holidays). My mom always went to church weekly; She would ask me weekly, "Did you go to church?" I would answer, "No, I don't have time." She would always say, "You make time for everything else; you could make time for church. It's only an hour." She was right about that, but, at the time, I wasn't thinking like that—until I started to go through some challenges with my own children. I started to have some worries and fear, and started to dwell on "what if." Some horrible thoughts would race through my head and try to take over me, but I did not allow them to. Cancel/Delete!

Society tries to brainwash you into believing you need to worry and fear. That is not truth; worrying and fearing does not help any situation. Taking action and having faith does. I would try my best to stay in faith. I felt like I had so many angels around me, and I would always pray for the angels to guard and protect all my children. When I was feeling down, I heard a whisper from my spirit to go to church. When I went to church I heard a message like it was directed to me, "We are all God's children, and your own children were gifted to you to nurture and love while on this earth." The tears flowed out of me and a peace came over me. Who better to watch over my children than God, the creator, father to all men and women? We are all his children. I learned to *let go and let God*. The burdens in my heart were released. When the heart opens up, tears pour out. I continue to go to church weekly to hear the messages I need to hear. My mom still asks me weekly if I went to church. Now I say, "Yes." A couple of messages I heard, that I felt I needed to share in this book are: "You will not be forgotten." That is truth. Walk in faith in the darkest moments, and you will find the light. There is nothing to ever fear but fear itself. Another message was, "Don't be fickle about your Faith." Don't depend on it sometimes, and at at other times, don't have the trust in it. Stay assured and confident. Having faith always works. Depend on it, all the time. Having a knowing it is already done.

When you learn the power of your thinking and how it has an effect on you and everything around you, you begin to really start paying attention. When I learned about this powerful secret, I felt it was my duty and obligation to bring this knowledge out for the benefit of you and all mankind. You will have a better night's sleep when you awaken your power within. A complete reassurance will come over you. Awaken faith so you could have the peace you deserve. God has our children in the palm of his hands and he has you in the palm of his hands. Pray on what you want God to help you with; be very specific, and talk in the positive. Talk and pray like it is already done. Breathe and release! That is Faith!

I have walked in faith since I was a young girl, and things always work out. About 25 years ago, I was driving to my mom and dad's home in Long Island. I was on the Southern State Pkwy with my three children, all under four years old. It was drizzling and gloomy out. I was driving in the third lane. We were going around a slight turn, and the car in front slowed down suddenly. I jammed on my brakes and my car did a total 360 spin, spiraling from the third lane all the way to the right side lane. I could not believe I did not hit one car, and no one hit me! I stopped on the side lane because I was totally shook up. Someone even stopped to see if we were ok, which I thought was very nice. Meanwhile, my son, Anthony, on the other hand, was laughing with delight; he thought it was so much fun. It was his perception, and his knowing—mommy would never do something that would hurt him. He felt secure. This is the same feeling God wants you to have. As soon as I saw all my children were fine, I thanked God and my angels. I knew I couldn't have gotten out of that safely on my own; I wasn't alone. Faith is a knowing that you are never alone—ever! I have been walking in faith for decades.

The enemies of faith are fears, doubts, and worries; they truly block your blessings without you even knowing it. With these negative thoughts, you magnetize things to you that you don't want: things that you have been thinking about, and how you don't want them to happen. I know that is a twist of words and may be hard for you to comprehend. You might be thinking, "If God wants to please me, why do all these negative things happen?" You might be saying: "I am a good person; I go to my house of worship every week; I help others." Honestly, those are great qualities, and that is a good starting point. It doesn't matter how good you are, how religious you are, what color you are, what your ethnic background is, or how rich or poor you are. Your capabilities of achieving does not discriminate against anyone. You all have equal chances of creating. There is success in all ethnic backgrounds. You have the same minutes in a day as everyone else. You are a child of God; you are a master creator. You have the Holy Spirit within you, breathing you. When you die, you leave your shell behind, and your spirit lives on.

Faith does not discriminate. Holding onto the actions and results of the past are discriminating. What is sad is the actual thought and belief of discrimination is what brings upon more discrimination. It's a vibrational pull, negative fueling negative, creating more negative results. You need to put that flame out. If you want discrimination to end, you have to stop thinking, writing, and talking about it. Think peace, write about peace, talk about peace and you will attract more peace. Think love, you will attract more love. Think gratitude, you will attract more gratitude. Think money, you will attract more money. Think happiness, you will attract more happiness. Think health, you will attract better health. This same philosophy goes with every single thing you think about in your life. If you want something, put all your thoughts, words, and energy on it. If you don't want something, refute it, and change the channel and cancel/delete any thoughts about it. Get out the eraser, and erase them from your thinking. Concentrate your thoughts on: "What would I Love?"

Awaken! Thank you, God! I have great faith in our great nation. I would like you to put your focus on world peace. I would like to strive towards it. I envision an independent nation, under God, indivisible, with liberty and justice for all. I am not political; I am spiritual, and I come with peace and love. I have a message that needs to be heard, loud and clear. Don't give up your power to anyone. Your power diminishes when you depend on others. Politics was taking the power away from the people and creating dependency. Trying to take power away from God, this nation was headed for disaster. Anyone full of greed and power for selfish reasons will be demolished. You need to take your power back. I feel Donald J. Trump must have asked God, "How can I help this great nation that is suffering?" God answered his prayers by calling upon him to help. God calls upon people on this earth to do his work. I believe President Donald J. Trump was called upon to save our great nation. My Intuition told me he was going to be President, once he was nominated. It was a calm and peaceful knowing. It doesn't need to make sense in the physical. Again, nothing to do with politics, it's spiritual. God does not always call the most qualified; he qualifies the call to action. President Trump is a master creator; he has been very successful most of his life. He was called upon to bring God back into your life and back into our nation. I have complete faith in President Donald J. Trump, and in our great nation under God. I hope you do too! Peace to the people of the world!

Like President Trump, I feel like I was called upon to write this book. It was never my desire to write a book, but it was my greatest desire to help the many that are suffering. I feel that through my decades of life and knowledge, I have many messages to share and I hope they will empower you. I kept asking God, "How can I get the messages out that I have learned through my years of life?" This book was the answer to my prayers, and I am very grateful it is complete. A few of the important messages are: Get rid of Fears, Doubts or Worriers, FEAR is False Evidence Appearing Real. Walk in Faith. *"The Power Within You is Greater Than Any Circumstance Around You."* Awaken your power if it is sleeping. Change your mindset to create better and better for yourself.

Repeat daily: "I am Getting Better and Better Every day in Every way." Have the Faith in knowing you are getting better. Take care of your *Royal Kingdom* with the *Royal Flush: Love, Oxygen, Water, Enzymes and Exercise!* . . . You O.W.E. it to yourself! "Say What you Want and Want What you Say". . . . I want this—"I Am Getting Tighter, Firmer and Sexier Every Day in Every Way!—Remember to have Fun! . . . LOL. Your Spirit loves fun!

When I listened to the loud voice inside to write this book, my F.E.E. to the Universe was that it had to be Fun, Easy, and Effortless. I agreed to do it. Everything is always an exchange of energy. I had total faith that God would keep his part of the bargain in guiding me to write this book—he did, and here it is. Done and ready for editing in less than six weeks, while living my normal busy life. There was nowhere in the physical realm that I would or could write a book. If you know me, I didn't even like writing a blog. My sister-in-law Toni was shocked when I told her I was writing a book. She reminded me, "You didn't even want to write a 1000 word essay for your holistic studies, term paper." This was true, I was stressing about that. This book is a reflection of the truth, and many messages that needed to be delivered. Don't make predictions in the physical, the spiritual realm is so much more: "With God, all things are Possible." I wrote a book! Wow! I'm still amazed! It feels surreal. If I could, you could! You could achieve anything you put your hearts desire on, no matter what circumstances look like and no matter what anyone else says.

Faith is knowing that your thoughts and beliefs will come to pass. Your thoughts dictate your feelings and become a vibrational pull to the actions that will occur, giving you the results that you have been putting your energy on, whether it be good or bad. *Like* attracts *like*. Positive thoughts attract positive results, and negative thoughts attract negative results. It's a Universal law. Things don't happen to you—they happen through you and with you. Peace be with you.

Your Kingdom, Your Power, and Your Glory are Yours, Now and Forever. . . . Amen!

POWER PAGE ... AMP UP YOUR POWER!

(Write Your Thoughts, Words and Affirmations)

_____

_____

_____

_____

_____

_____

_____

_____

_____

_____

_____

_____

_____

_____

_____

_____

_____

_____

_____

_____

_____

_____

Made in the USA
Middletown, DE
05 May 2017